Tough thread-sewn bi[nding] and flexi cover

The tough thread-sew[n...] flexible cover allow th[...] ded right back on its [...] you to keep your plac[...] you use it on your wa[lk...]

Information boxes – getting to and from each walk

The information boxes give an overview of the route and include everything you need to know for planning and logistics: getting to and from the walk by public transport or in your own car, places to eat and drink along the way and any special clothing or equipment required.

Warning: mountain walking can be dangerous

Every effort has been made by the author and publishers to ensure that the information contained herein is as accurate and up to date as possible. However, they are unable to accept responsibility for any inconvenience, loss or injury sustained by anyone as a result of the advice and information given in this guide. Nature and the climate ultimately remain unpredictable elements. The condition of paths and trails always depends on the time, weather conditions, human interventions and other unforeseeable events. Note the safety warning below. We ask for your understanding, and welcome any suggestions for improvements.

For your safety

Do not overestimate your abilities – you're on holiday, so relax and enjoy it! You'll find that all routes on Madeira are beautiful, including those marked with just one or two stars. Take particular care when walking on levada paths, including the easier ones – accidents only occur here through carelessness. Avoid walking alone if possible but, if you do, inform someone from your group or the hotel of your plans and take sufficient drinking water and your mobile phone (though not all mountainous areas enjoy good reception). Trail sections, and particularly those in narrow ravines, can remain muddy and slippery for long periods after rainfall.

In the event of an emergency, dial 📞 **112** (EU-wide emergency number) or 📞 **291-700112** (Serviço Proteção Civil, the Madeiran Civil Protection Service)

MADEIRA
WALKS

Oliver Breda

😊 child-friendly walks

■ Text and research: Oliver Breda ■ Translation: Joseph France ■ Editors and proofreaders (English edition) Celia Marshall-Bingler, Jane Thomas and Daniel McCrohan ■ Series concept: Michael Müller, Angela Nitsche, Hana Gundel, Dirk Thomsen ■ Editing: Angela Nitsche ■ Layout: Michael Müller ■ Maps: Janina Baumbauer, Benedikt Neuwirth, Inger Holndonner ■ GPS mapping: Hauke Hoppe-Seyler ■ GIS consulting: Rolf Kastner ■ Climate data analysis: Steffen Fietze ■ Route-time-elevation diagrams: Janina Baumbauer, Inger Holndonner ■ Photos: Oliver Breda ■ Cover design: Karl Serwotka ■ Cover photo: In the Nuns' Valley (Walk 21) ■

Co-published 2018 by Michael Müller Verlag (Germany) and Trailblazer Publications (UK)

ISBN 978-1-905864-99-7

If you have any suggestions for amendments, improvements or tips to add to this book, let us know!
Write to us at: info@trailblazer-guides.com

1st English edition, 2018

Walking on Madeira

▶ Like a garden floating in the Atlantic, Madeira blooms year round with a diverse range of flora from all over the world, and there's lush greenery even in the dry season from July to September. Yet the island offers so much more than this: aficionados of wild, rugged landscapes will also

find all they could wish for in a perfect walking destination. The island features a jagged landscape with steep valleys and an indented coastline.

Madeira does indeed have something for everyone: from pleasant strolls along the levadas, the island's unique irrigation channels, to challenging walks of an Alpine character.

In this walking guide, I have selected a range of routes that should enable everyone to explore the variety of landscapes on offer on the island of Madeira. ■

Walking regions

Madeira can be roughly divided into five areas that correspond to the different walking regions in this book (south-east, north-east, central region, south-west and north-west).

▶ **South-east (p. 32–61) and south-west (p. 142–175):** The south of the island is densely populated up to about 600 m, and is criss-crossed by numerous roads and tunnels. At first sight, it might seem surprising that Madeira also has unspoilt nature to offer – but it does. In the south-east, the island is mainly dry and windy (Walk 1) though walkers must also contend with rain and fog at elevations above 500 m to 600 m (Walk 3). Farming concentrates on field crops such as onions or potatoes, though sugar cane is also grown in some of the more humid valleys (Walk 2). The south-west is dominated by deeply cut valleys: the Ribeira Brava (Walks 28 and 21) and Ponta do Sol (Walks 29 and 30) are particularly impressive examples. Between Funchal and Calheta, bananas, sugar cane, and in some places tropic fruits abound – no wonder, as the south-west region across to Funchal is the warmest part of the island, and also features numerous levadas. Though the island's interior is less rugged in the west, the coast still features impressive cliff landscapes (Walk 31). ■

> **Caution**
>
> The paths through the mountains and by the coast are clearly laid out. However, following a direct route or walking cross-country simply isn't possible on Madeira: the island is too steep and the rock too brittle. Even experienced mountain hikers should not underestimate Madeira's wild nature. You should also take care when following maps from OpenStreetMap, as not all of the paths shown can be safely negotiated.

▶ **Central region (p. 94–141):** The island's interior consists of two entirely different landscapes: on the one hand, there are the jagged, rugged central mountains with the island's highest peaks, bizarre rock formations (Walks 16 and 17) and vast erosion craters, such as the Nuns' Valley (Walks 18, 19, 20 and 21), while on the other hand there is the flat and relatively barren Paúl da Serra plateau (Walk 23 and 26). ■

▶ **North-east (p. 62–93) and north-west (p. 176–201):** The entire northern part of the island is steeper, less densely populated and more wild. Quite often – but primarily in elevated areas above 600 m – conditions can become humid and cloudy, though the area can be sunny and warm in south-westerly winds. The north-east boasts fascinating deep, dark green valleys with steep sides and towering waterfalls (Walks 11, 13 and 14). Large parts of the north-west are barely accessible, and only a few routes allow walkers to explore the area's unspoilt landscape (Walks 33 and 34). The spectacular ecosystem of the laurel forest can be explored intensively on Walks 36 and 37. ■

You can find the best locations for each route on p. 22.

▶ Weather and seasons: Madeira is renowned for its balanced, spring-like climate which it enjoys all year round. This is particularly true for the lower parts of the south coast; though the island may be relatively small (about 740 km²), its rugged, jagged landscape

Weather and the walking season

is subject to significant regional differences. From January to April, it's not at all unusual to experience four seasons in one day: summer on the south-west coast, spring in bloom at moderate elevations (200–400 m), autumn with wind, rain and cloud at higher altitudes and winter with ice and snow in the summit region.

July, August and September are the warmest months, with average temperatures of about 22°C in Funchal (→ Table of average daily temperatures) and almost 15°C on the highest peaks. July is the driest month: a cloud belt often forms around the island then, and it rarely if ever sees rainfall, while the summit region is largely cloudless.

Most rainfall occurs as localised showers from October to March (→ Table of rainfall), though days where the entire island sees rainfall are rare. Madeira rarely suffers from thunderstorms. ■

▶ Wind conditions: A north-easterly wind (north-east trade wind) generally blows onto the island almost all year round, if it is not

Daylight hours on Madeira				
Day	Sunrise	Sunset	Longest possible daylight duration	
	(Local time)	(Local time)	Funchal	Man-chester
15 Jan.	8.09	18.24	10:15 hrs	8:03 hrs
15 Feb.	7.52	18.52	11:00 hrs	9:52 hrs
15 Mar.	7.19	19.14	11:55 hrs	11:00 hrs
15 April	7.38	20.37	12:59 hrs	14:01 hrs
15 May	7.09	20.59	13:50 hrs	15:54 hrs
15 June	6.59	21.16	14:17 hrs	17:00 hrs
15 July	7.10	21.16	14:06 hrs	16:30 hrs
15 Aug.	7.30	20.54	13:24 hrs	14:48 hrs
15 Sep.	7.50	20.16	12:26 hrs	12:41 hrs
15 Oct.	8.11	19.36	11:25 hrs	10:36 hrs
15 Nov.	7.37	18.07	10:30 hrs	8:37 hrs
15 Dec.	8.02	18.04	10:02 hrs	7:30 hrs

Greenwich Mean Time (GMT) is observed on Madeira (GMT + 1 in summer) so there is no time difference between Madeira and UK. Funchal: 32° 39' northern latitude, 16° 54' western longitude. Manchester: 53° 29' northern latitude.

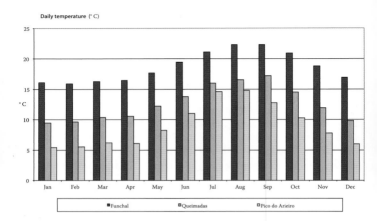

Daily temperature (° C)

■Funchal   ▫Queimadas   ▫Pico do Arieiro

replaced by any of the winds detailed below. The north-east trade wind condenses to fog along the north coast above about 800 m and sometimes sweeps over the main ridge to the south side. Obviously, only higher areas are affected.

Wind from the north-west often cools the island, bringing cold rain to the north coast, the extreme south-west, the Paúl da Serra plateau and the summit region, though the south-east generally escapes this rainfall.

Wind from the south-west can result in heavy showers across the south of the island, at high altitudes and in the summit region. The north-east usually escapes such showers, as does the south-east.

Wind from the east/south-east is known as the 'Leste'. This hot wind descends on Madeira, drying out the air within a few hours and causing temperatures to rise rapidly. In rainy seasons, walkers couldn't ask for anything better – but in summer, the Leste means that even shorts can feel too much, though this hot, dry wind rarely persists for long. ■

▶ **Walking season:** Walkers can explore all regions of Madeira throughout the year. Rain and fog can occur all year round, though such conditions are generally localised and temporary.

Temperatures in autumn, winter and spring are ideal for walking. Although routes through the central mountains and across the plateau might not be feasible at specific times, walkers will not have to wait long for the next suitable day. The major plus in winter months is the island's long days (→ Table p. 9). While it might be getting dark back at home, the light means walkers can continue to explore Madeira. Having said that, it's important to remember that some narrow valleys can become dark long before the sun sets.

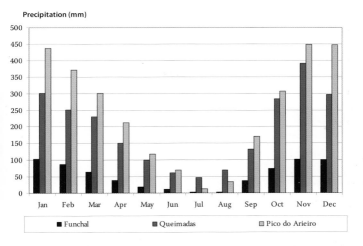

Precipitation (mm)

■ Funchal   ■ Queimadas   ▣ Pico do Arieiro

Summer is not too warm, and offers perfect walking conditions at high altitudes. Very few walks in central and lower areas are entirely without shade (Walk 1 is one of the exceptions), so walkers can roam across the entire island during the summer. ■

Let's start with the most important thing for walkers on Madeira to remember: the rock is brittle! Though the ground may appear solid, don't be tempted to stray too close to a precipice.

Geology for walkers

▶ Volcanic activity: Madeira is an entirely volcanic island, and was not created through geological folds or tectonic uplifts. As a result, plutonic rocks like granite, crystalline shale or sedimentary rocks such as those found in the Limestone Alps – relatively solid rock types well-known to alpine walkers and which can bear their weight – are not found on the island. Indeed, almost all of Madeira is composed of tuff, basalt and trachyte (see below), built up in irregular layers.

It is thought that the last volcanic eruption here occurred 400,000 years ago. There was no central volcano, and the island was instead formed by numerous smaller eruptions and 'gentle' volcanic fissures: indeed, the bizarre peaks in the island's interior are the solidified vents of the individual volcanoes. The mountain surrounding them has simply been eroded away over the course of millennia, leaving behind a striking landscape of former volcanoes in the central mountainous region (→ Walks 16 and 17). Walkers can get very close to a former volcanic vent on Walk 22.

The rest of the volcanic fissures are now flat stone surfaces that look like walls in the landscape, a beautiful example of which can be visited on Walk 17. Other such stone walls which have not been completely weathered out can be found at the eastern tip (→ Walk 1). ∎

▶ **Tuff** is formed by explosive volcanic eruptions and is nothing more than ash compacted into solid rock by wind, weather and overlying stone layers. The outer surface is usually rough, and does not become

The levadas: Madeira's lifelines

The first Portuguese settlers in the first half of the 15th century tapped springs and streams to irrigate their fields. As early as 1461, officials were employed to monitor this water distribution system and, as the centuries went by, the network of open irrigation channels became increasingly sophisticated.

The principle is quite simple: collection levadas run at a height of 800 m to 1,300 m, where water is collected from various springs, streams and rivers. The levadas usually end at large downspouts where the water falls to the next level. The water then flows through a hydroelectric power station and is then channelled to the irrigation levadas, which run at an altitude of 400 m to 600 m. It is crucial that they run as flat as possible, as only the land beneath the levada can be watered. The island's fields and farmlands are irrigated in accordance with a precise annual schedule. The entire year is divided into hours, which can be rented by farmers. More affluent farmers tend to have a cistern which they fill during their allotted hours, while the less well-off have to water their fields during their rented hours.

Major levada construction work was carried out in the 16th century, as sugar cane production required large quantities of water. In the 19th century, the water supply on the south side of the island subsequently became insufficient. Sources in the north had to be tapped and water transported to the south side through tunnels. The levada system at Rabaçal (→ Walk 25) dates from this period, as does the Levada do Furão at Ribeiro Frio (→ Walk 10). Many new levadas and several hydroelectric power stations were created in a further major construction period from 1939 to 1969, including the Levada do Norte (→ Walk 27) which, when full, can transport about 1,000 litres per second.

The generally well-maintained levada system has created ideal paths for walkers; at times, these paths run along gentle slopes (→ Walk 31), but are generally on firm ground and are often in the vertical wall (→ Walk 30). The levadas make it possible to reach areas by foot that would otherwise be completely inaccessible (→ Walks 8, 13, 14, 24 and 25). However, you must keep your wits about you when walking as the seemingly easy paths are sometimes anything but.

Summit path to Pico Ruivo (Walk 17)

slippery when wet. However, heavily weathered tuff is like ice when wet, and such surfaces are encountered along some of the levadas. You should take particular care in such areas as tuff is easily eroded: it can sometimes be crumbled away by hand, hence the warning at the start of this section. However, steps can also be cut into tuff faces that would otherwise barely be accessible (→ Walk 17).

The tuff rock on Madeira is ferrous and porous; the various red colourations are caused by the rock's different oxidation states. Delightful colours and weird formations can be seen in the rocks at the eastern tip (→ Walk 1). ■

▶ **Basalt and trachyte** are the products of volcanic eruptions with slow-flowing lava. These related rocks are very hard and grey in colour. Trachyte has a higher proportion of quartz, but only basalt can form five-edged columns in the direction the lava cools. Basalt and trachyte both become very slippery when wet so take care on walks involving natural stone steps composed of these rocks. ■

▶ **Phonolite** is another rock related to basalt and trachyte that appears less frequently on Madeira. On first glance, it's hard to distinguish it from basalt or trachyte: it breaks into flat shards and needle-like rocks. One distinctive characteristic of phonolite is its sound, as the flat, thin shards sound like breaking glass when walked on (→ Walk 17 when climbing from the saddle of the Pico das Torres towards Pico Ruivo and Walk 21 when climbing along the stone wall). ■

Flora

Madeira's promotionally effective sobriquet, the 'floating garden in the Atlantic', is certainly apt, with plants from all over the world thriving in this small space. The avenues and gardens are a blaze of vibrant colours, with owners keen to plant new tropical and subtropical species. The island's native coastal vegetation is characterised by thick-leaved stonecrops that enjoy the dry conditions. Levadas often lead through arable land with terraced fields where native vegetation has been displaced, though flowers often line the paths.

The laurel forest at altitudes between 600 m and 1,300 m is typical vegetation for Madeira, and this is where the island's native flora is best preserved. Above this level are the mountains. The significant variations in temperature over the course of a day make big demands on plant life. Due to the wealth of local flora, I can only mention a small selection of the most common or special plants. For further information see *Madeira – A Botanical Melting Pot!* (available in Engish or German from www.bredaverlag.de).

▶ **Plants in gardens and avenues:** The Avenida Arriaga in Funchal is lined with jacaranda trees, which grow to about 20 m tall and lose their leaves in winter. Before the tree sprouts new leaves, it produces striking violet blossoms in April and May. The African tulip tree (Spathodea campanulata) is also a common sight in squares and streets, especially in Funchal. It also grows to a height of 20–25 m, but flowers year round. Its leaves are dark green, while its orange-red flowers are reminiscent of tulips. Many gardens feature angel's trumpets (Brugmansia aurea), which also flower all year and have now become a popular tub plant in mainland Europe. This shrub can reach a height of about 4 m, with long blooms reminiscent of the wind instrument, but beware: all parts of this plant are poisonous! By

Madeira blueberry   Lily-of-the-valley tree

contrast, hibiscus hedges are ubiquitous and harmless, and bloom all year round in a wide range of colours. The bird of paradise flower (Strelitzia reginae) has almost become a Madeiran emblem and, though expensive in garden centres back home, they are used here to decorate motorway embankments and traffic islands. They flower all year round, but mainly in winter and springtime. ■

▶ Crop plants: Field terraces with bananas are omnipresent between Funchal and Calheta. Large plantations are rare on Madeira, and instead crops are grown on terraces that are not always connected to one another. The bananas cultivated on the island are dwarf bananas which grow on smaller shrubs more resistant to the wind. The most common crop in previous centuries was sugar cane, grown by the first settlers over 500 years ago. This 'white gold' once brought great wealth to the island. Some sugar cane fields can still be found today in the south-west. Though vines are a common sight across the island, don't expect to see extensive vineyards – Madeira only started to produce table wine a few years ago. Most grapes are grown for the famous fortified Madeira wine. ■

▶ Coastal vegetation: Though once a common sight in the wild, today most of the dragon trees (Dracaena) have been planted by hand. The botanic garden in Funchal boasts some magnificent specimens. At Ponta São Lourenço, an area above the Prainha beach has been reforested with small dragon trees. The massaroco (Echium nervosum) also grows at Ponta São Lourenço (→ Walk 1). This shrub can grow up to about 1 m in height, with striking compact, candle-shaped violet flowerheads, and flowers from January to April. Barren hillsides on the island's dry south coast are often home to succulent smooth spear-leaved spurge (Euphorbia piscadoria). This densely branched bush has slender, blue-green leaves that it sheds in spring, before sprouting new leaves in autumn. The plant's sap is poisonous and, in the past, was used to stun fish to render them easier to catch in shallow water. These hillsides also often feature the prickly pear (Opuntia ficus-indica), a plant well-known in the Mediterranean. In September, their blossoms develop prickly, edible fruit. Another unusual plant is the crystalline ice plant (Mesembryanthemum crystallinum), which grows at the Ponta de São Lourenço (→ Walk 1). This plant, the leaves of which are edible, only reaches a height of 10–20 cm and has white to pink flowers from April to June. When the sun catches the plant at the

Pride of Madeira

right angle, it appears to be covered in ice crystals, though these are in fact water vesicles on its leaves and stem. Along roadsides, on fallow land and in gardens, aloe vera is a common sight. The leaves are reminiscent of agaves, with serrated edges and grow to 30 cm long. From December to June, aloe vera plants produce flower heads up to 80 cm height, with yellow tubular flowers. On Madeira, the plant is used to produce a healing gel that can be purchased in almost every supermarket. ■

▶ **Flora along the levadas:** The slopes along the southern coast, where the majority of levadas are situated, have been systematically dug up and terraced ever since settlement began in Madeira. As agriculture lost its importance, many areas and fields lay idle, and work to reforest the area began under the Salazar dictatorship in the 20th century. The predominant vegetation is a mixed woodland composed of eucalyptus, acacia and cluster pine, all fast-growing trees. Levada wardens planted hydrangeas and African lilies (Agapanthus praecox) not only for aesthetic reasons, but also because their roots served to reinforce pathways. In the island's humid valleys, calla lilies grow almost like weeds. The same can be said for the common hedgenettle, which looks like a daisy and is said to possess medicinal and magical powers. ■

▶ **Flora of the laurel forest:** Four species of laurel thrive on the island of Madeira, the most striking being stinkwood (til; Ocotea foetens). This tree is happiest at a height of 1,100 m to 1,500 m and can grow up to 40 m tall. Its trunk is often gnarled and covered with mosses, lichens and ferns, and while its leaves are the typical laurel shape, its berries are reminiscent of acorns. Some splendid specimens can be found beneath the Pico Grande, between the Encumeada pass and Boca do Cerro (→ Walk 21). The mighty trees at Fanal (→ Walk 37) are certainly impressive. The northern slopes of the Encumeada pass (→ Walk 36) have extensive and dense laurel forests.

The **Canary laurel** (Laurus novocanariensis) is more slender, and only grows up to a height of 25 m. It is also often bush-shaped, with numerous stems from one rootstock. This plant prefers higher altitudes between 1,000 m and 1,400 m; it has typical laurel-shape leaves larger than those of the stinkwood and bears fruit that look like olives. Its leaves are the only ones suitable for use as seasoning.

Madeira laurel (Persea indica) is another of the island's laurel species. It too can be found in the narrow valleys of the south coast and in altitudes of up to 500 m; the tree grows to be 15–25 m tall, with leaves up to 20 cm long and fruit reminiscent of tiny avocados. Older leaves turn red before they fall.

The fourth member of the island's laurel family is the **Canary laurel, also known as barbusano** (Apollonias barbujana). It rarely grows at altitudes above 700 m, and reaches a height of 10–20 m. With its leaves often curled at the edges, it can usually be found in the Ribeira do Tristão valley (→ Walk 35).

Stinkwood

The laurel forest zone (→ Box, Walk 3) from 600 to 1,500 m altitude is characterised by high humidity levels. As a result, the trees are often covered with long beard lichen (Usnea barbata). Large ferns, such as the European chain fern (Woodwardia radicans), populate the rock faces with imposing, feather-like fronds of up to 3 m in length. The humid, northern side is home to the lily-of-the-valley tree (Clethra arborea), which only grows to be 7 m high and has flowers (from July to September) rather like those of its smaller namesake. You can see them in the Ribeiro Frio area (→ Walks 10 and 11). ■

The calla lily – a frequent inhabitant of humid valley floors

▶ Flora in the mountains: The massive tree heaths (Erica arborea) between Pico das Torres and Pico Ruivo (→ Walk 17) are very imposing. They grow up to 5 m with a thick trunk, and produce inconspicuous white flowers from March to May. Some of the older trees fell victim to a serious fire in 2010, though many rootstocks have begun to sprout again. Another famous example of the island's flora is the Pride of Madeira (Echium fastuosum), an endemic species of bugloss only found here. It is similar to the massaroco found in coastal regions (see above). However, the flower heads are slimmer and feature more densely-packed, dark-violet blooms. The shrub grows to a height of about 1.50 m and thrives at altitudes above 800 m. Numerous specimens grow on the road from Ribeira Brava to the Encumeada pass. Another curious species is the Madeira blueberry (Vaccinium padifolium). This shrub grows several metres tall, and its fruits (August to October) are similar to the familiar blueberry and are also edible. Many bushes grow in the shadows of laurel trees along the Levada do Furado (→ Walk 10). Another interesting specimen is the Madeiran yellow violet (Viola paradoxa), often found around Pico Arieiro (→ Walk 17). An equally common species is the branching orchid (Orchis scopulorum), which flourishes on the rock faces between Pico do Arieiro and Pico Ruivo (→ Walk 17) and on the path from Lombo do Mouro to Pináculo (→ Walk 22), as well as in the vicinity of Ribeiro Frio (→ Walks 10 and 11). ■

Fauna

By comparison with the broad range of flora, fauna on the island is somewhat limited. Madeira is situated far into the Atlantic, meaning that only species that can fly or swim made it to the island without assistance from humans.

▶ **Fauna on land and in the air:** Before the arrival of man on the island, the only native mammals were **bats**. In the early 15th century, the first settlers brought cows, sheep, pigs, goats, rabbits, dogs, cats and hens with them. Like everywhere else, mice and rats were also in tow. **Wall lizards** and **wall geckos** arrived on ships and flotsam. There are no **snakes** on the island.

Birdlife is rather more diverse. **Buzzards** often circle the valleys, while **kestrels** (Falco tinnunculus) are also native to the island. With any luck, in the evenings and at night you might encounter a **barn owl** (Tyto alba) out hunting.

The laurel forest is home to the shy **Madeira laurel pigeon** (Columba trocaz): this species is endemic, meaning that it is only found on Madeira, and grows up to 40 cm. You can often find it along the seldom-used Caminho do Norte (Walk 36). Its counterpart is the tiny and also endemic **Madeira firecrest** (Regulus madeirensis), which only measures 8 cm when fully grown. Walkers in the Ribeira da Janela valley (→ Walk 34) or on the Ribeiro Frio trail (→ Walks 10 and 11) have the best chance of seeing this bird. The **Madeira chaffinch** (Fringilla coelebs madeirensis) is a common sight, and is almost irritatingly friendly at popular spots for a break, while the **wagtails**, with their bobbing flight, are rather more reserved.

The **Atlantic canary** (Serinus canaria), an ancestor of the famous yellow domestic canary, can be found in lower, coastal areas. In the wild, however, the species is an inconspicuous greenish-brown colour, and only the adult males' breasts display a bright greenish-yellow splash of colour.

Madeira chaffinch

As the Atlantic surrounding Madeira is very deep (up to 3,000 m) with relatively few fish, seabirds are less common than you might otherwise expect. The **Cory's shearwater** (Calonectris diomedea) and **Madeiran storm petrel** (Oceanodroma castro), which flit just above the surface of the water, are common ocean-going birds. A less common sight is the **Bulwer's petrel** (Bulweria bulwerii). One of the rarest ocean-going bird species is the endemic **Madeira petrel** (Pterodroma madeira), which is at risk of extinction. Some pairs nest in the vicinity of Pico do Arieiro along the closed path through the tunnel (→ Walk 17).

Madeira is thought to be home to about 2,000 species of insect, all of which are more or less harmless – only the **burrowing wasps** become aggressive when disturbed. It is perhaps worth highlighting the **monarch butterflies** (Danaus plexippus): their orange wings with dark edges can grow to a span of up to 10 cm.

Ticks are prevalent in the pasture areas, though whether they also transmit diseases on Madeira is not known. ∎

▶ **Aquatic fauna:** Various whale species, including dolphins, occasionally pass by Madeira. One particular highlight is a small colony of **Mediterranean monk seals** (Monachus monachus), which live on the Desertas Islands to the south of Madeira.

The **black scabbardfish** (Aphanopus carbo) lives at depths of around 1,500 m, and so can only be found in restaurants, supermarkets and at markets. Its body is long, slender and black, while its head with fang-like teeth certainly looks threatening. These fish are caught at night with kilometre-long fishing lines, but the fish dies as a result of the large drop in pressure when being hauled in, and it is said that no human has seen one alive. **Tuna** are relatively common in the waters around Madeira. **Limpets** (Patellidae), which cling to rockfaces below the waterline, are fried and served with lemon juice and garlic (Port.: Lapas) on Madeira. To the chagrin of local fishermen, **gilthead sea bream** are almost exclusively reared in fish farms, with pools anchored around Madeira. The waters around Madeira are also home to several small species of shark. In Câmara de Lobos, **catsharks** are sometimes used as stockfish. ∎

Limpets in the market hall at Funchal

▶ No special equipment is required when walking on Madeira, and standard clothing is sufficient: ankle-high, non-slip walking shoes, sun and rain protection, and possibly walking poles for steep ascents

Equipment and provisions

and descents, or to aid balance on the levada walls. However, be sure to take warm clothes whatever the season: long trousers, a jumper or fleece jacket and wind-proof jacket. Some routes lead through levada tunnels, which can only be traversed with a torch. A day pack is sufficient for all of the walks in this book.

The best non-slip footwear

In my opinion, mid-weight walking shoes made by Lowa, Meindl, Hanwag or Mammut are worth considering. In any case, the sole should not be too hard. Vibram soles are good. Truly non-slip shoes can be found at a specialist workwear retailer, where shoes for construction workers have had their grip qualities tested. The downside is that such shoes are often less suitable for walking, and can hurt your feet after only a few hours.

Of course, the type and quantity of trail snacks you choose to take is up to you — but make sure to bring plenty of drinking water, as on more demanding walks, and in higher temperatures, a walker can lose up to a litre of fluid per hour. The water in the levadas in the inhabited area is not drinking water; you should also avoid drinking from levadas in the mountains. ∎

▶ A mobile phone is useful in case of emergencies (make sure it's fully charged); the mobile network on Madeira is well developed, and dead spots are rare.

Emergencies and emergency numbers

Mountain rescue duties on Madeira are undertaken by the fire brigade (Bombeiros). For emergency calls, dial the national emergency number ☎ 112, and you will be transferred accordingly (also operates in English).

Alternatively, you can turn to the Civil Protection Service on Madeira (Serviço Proteção Civil) at ☎ 291-700112 (also in English), which also responds in rescue and emergency situations.

The Portuguese telephone network no longer recognises prefixes, so the nine-figure telephone numbers, which usually start with ☎ 291 on Madeira, must be dialled in full.

If you have travelled with a tour operator, in an emergency you should contact your tour guide. Many operators have a specific emergency number.

Almost all small towns have health centres (Centro de Saúde) which can treat minor injuries. ∎

▶ **Hospitals:** Hospital Regional Cruz Carvalho, Avenida Luis Camões, Funchal, ✆ 291-705600; public hospital.

Clínica de Santa Catarina, Rua de 5 de Outubro 115, Funchal, ✆ 291-700000, 24/7 emergency number at ✆ 291-745780; private clinic.

Clínica de Santa Luzia, Rua da Torinha 5, Funchal, ✆ 291-200000; private clinic, good care, but expensive.

Policlinica do Caniço, Rua Dr. F. Peres, Caniço, ✆ 291-934504, ✆ 291-930070; public doctor's surgery. ■

Route planning

The walking routes in this guide require a certain degree of preparation. The timings given are for walking time without breaks. If you're a keen photographer, like to take in the landscape or enjoy stopping for breaks at scenic spots, you may need more time. It's always advisable to start a walk early in the day (→ Table of sunrise and sunset times and daylight hours on p. 9). Due to its geographic location, dusk is a rather short period in comparison to central and northern Europe. In narrow valleys, it can become quite dark before the sun sets.

▶ **Locations:** If you decide to rent a car, you can base yourself anywhere you wish on Madeira. The road network is well developed, and makes it possible to visit the entire island. It is not strictly necessary to stay in different locations. If you opt to use public transport to get around the island, the best option is to choose accommodation in central Funchal.

> **Tip**
>
> In cooler months, you should make sure that accommodation above 400 m has heating in all rooms.

South-east: The most popular destination in the south-east is Caniço de Baixo, which has numerous hotels and apartment complexes. The tourist infrastructure (restaurants, cafés, bars) is good, with frequent bus connections to Funchal and the east of the island.

Machico, the island's oldest town, has hotels and guest houses, as well as a lovely city beach. The town is still overwhelmingly local but is fairly quiet in the evenings. There are relatively good bus connections to the north-east of the island. Reaching other parts with public transport can be problematic.

Funchal is not only the island's capital (about 125,000 inhabitants) but is also its most popular destination. Despite this, the city is relatively peaceful and relaxed, and has retained its traditional Portuguese charm. The city centre has a good range of guest houses, apartments and hotels to suit all tastes and budgets, while there are also plenty of restaurants, cafés and bars, etc. The hotel district lies to the west of

the historical centre, and offers a little more hustle-and-bustle. The accommodation consists predominantly of 4- to 5-star hotels. City buses provide regular connections to the centre. If you wish to explore the island by bus, taking a bus into the city centre is recommended. Almost all intercity buses stop there.

South-west: Ribeira Brava enjoys good transport links and a good infrastructure (restaurants, cafés, supermarkets, shops, bathing area by the sea). In the evenings, the locals tend to keep to themselves.

Ponta do Sol is a small, picturesque town with two hotels. There are good bus connections to Ribeira Brava and the west of the island, though travellers must change in Ribeira Brava and Funchal to reach other regions.

There is some accommodation in the vicinity of **Calheta**, but a rental car is an advantage. In Vila da Calheta, there is even a sandy beach.

North: The north is less populated, and is more wild than the south coast. Bus connections to the north are mainly based on locals' needs, and so a rental car is advisable. Key locations for walkers are **São Vicente**, with good bus connections to the south coast, as well as **Santana** and **Porto Moniz** with its large ocean swimming pool.

Centre: Some places in the mountains (e.g. Residencial Encumeada → Walk 21, Hotel Pico da Urze → Walk 23) offer guests transfers to nearby walking routes. However, as there are not enough routes in the area to keep most walkers occupied, a change of location is recommended.■

► **Tourist information from home**

Turismo de Portugal, www.visitpor tugal.com, ✆ 020 7201 6633 (UK). In addition, www.visit-madeira.pt, specific to Madeira, includes a list of all officially marked walking routes. ∎

► **Tourist information on the island**

Funchal

Posto de Turismo, 9004-519 Funchal, Av. Arriaga 16, ✆ 291-211902, open Mon-Fri 9am–7pm, Sat/Sun & bank hols until 3pm: Madeira's main office, well equipped. Information on accommo-dation, bus connections, sights; also sells books and maps. Most staff speak English, and sometimes German. 9004-519 Funchal, Av. Arriaga 16, ✆ 291-211902, open 9am–7pm Mon-Fri, Sat/Sun and bank hols until 3pm: Madeira's main office, well equipped. Information on accommodation, bus connections, sights; also sells books and maps. Most staff speak English; some also speak other languages.

Curral das Freiras

Posto de Informação Turística, 9030-319 Curral das Freiras, Estrada Cónego Camacho, ✆ 291-721183, Weds & Thurs 9.30am–3.30pm.

Machico

Posto de Turismo, 9200 Machico, Forte Nossa Senhora do Amparo, ✆ 291-962289, open (not Sun) 9am–12.30pm & 2pm–5pm, Sat only until 12pm.

Ribeira Brava

Posto de Turismo, 9350 Ribeira Brava, Forte de São Bento, ✆ 291-951675, open (not Sun) 10am–3.30pm, Sat until 12.30pm: Information primarily regard-ing Ribeira Brava area and the south-west.

It's not only walkers that enjoy the view from Rabaçal (Walk 25)

Santana

Posto de Turismo, 9230 Santana, Sítio do Serrado, in a thatched house by the town hall, ☎ 291-572992, open (not Sun) 10am–1pm and 2pm–5.30pm, Sat only until 12pm: Information on the north.

Porto Moniz

Posto de Turismo, 9270 Porto Moniz, opposite 'Piscinas Naturais', ☎ 291-853075, Mon 11am–3pm, Tue–Fri 11am–3.30pm, Sat 12pm–3pm: Information on the north. ∎

▶ **Taxi:** The taxis in Funchal have meters which must be switched on for urban journeys. Taxis outside Funchal rarely have meters, and bear an 'A' on the doors. Fixed prices exist for journeys between towns; each driver must carry a list of these prices with them. As a rough guide, prices are €0.63/km plus a base charge of about €4; a 20% surcharge is added for 6-seater taxis and at the weekend. Vouchers for costlier journeys can be booked in advance at www.aitram.pt. ∎

▶ **Bus:** The localities between Ribeira Brava and Machico along the south coast are relatively well connected. However, journey times are lengthened by the numerous stops. Intercity buses on Madeira are operated by four bus companies.

▶ **Bus departure times for walking routes:** The times given below are specifically selected for each walk, so that you can get by without a bus timetable. Of course, changes are always possible. The bus companies all have reliable websites giving the individual timetables for each bus line.

Walk 1

Out: Line 113 (SAM) Funchal – Caniçal – Baía D'Abra, from Funchal Mon–Fri 7.30, 8.30, 9.00, 11.30, 12.15, 14.30, Sat 7.30, 8.30, 9.00, 10.30, 11.30, 12.15, 14.30, Sun 7.30, 9.00, 10.30, 11.30, 15.00. Journey approx. 1:30 hr.

Return: Line 113 (SAM) Baía D'Abra – Caniçal – Funchal, from Baía D'Abra Mon–Fri 10.30, 11.30, 12.00, 12.55, 13.55, 15.00, 16.00, 17.00, 18.15, 19.35 (May to Oct), Sat 10.30, 11.30, 13.00, 14.00, 17.00, 18.15, 19.35 (May to Oct), Sun 11.55, 14.00, 17.00, 18.15.

Walk 2

Out: Line 156 (SAM) Funchal – Maroços, from Funchal Mon–Fri 6.45, 8.00, Sat 6.45, 8.00, Sun and bank hols 12.15. Line 208 (SAM) Funchal – Maroços – Porto da Cruz, from Funchal Mon–Fri 10.30, 11.45, Sat, Sun and bank hols only from Santa Cruz 11.00 and Machico 11.20. Line 156 (SAM) from Machico Mon–Sat 8.50, Sun and bank hols 8.00, 10.30 and 13.15. Line 208 (SAM) also from Machico 11.20.

Return: Line 113 (SAM) Caniçal – Funchal, from Caniçal Mon–Fri 12.05, 13.00, 14.00, 15.05, 16.05, 17.05, 18.25 and 19.40. Journey from Caniçal, stopping at the end of the walk, is 15–20mins.

Walk 3

Out: Line 53 (SAM) Funchal – Portela – Faial, from Funchal Mon–Fri 10.00, 13.15, Sat 10.00, 13.15, from Machico Mon–Fri 9.00, 10.50, Sat 9.00 and 10.50.

Return: Line 53 (SAM) Faial – Portela – Funchal, from Faial Mon–Fri 13.10, 15.40, 17.15, 18.20, Sat 15.40, 17.45, Sun and bank hols only 10.15. Journey to the Portela pass approx. 20 mins.

Walk 4

Out: Line 77 to 4 Estradas (CCSG), Funchal – Santo da Serra (via 4 Estradas) from Funchal Mon–Fri 7.35, 10.30, 14.00, Sat 7.40, 10.30, 14.00, Sun 8.30, 10.30, 14.00.

Return: Line 53 (SAM), Faial – Funchal (via Portela and Machico), from Faial Mon–Fri 13.10, 15.40, 17.15, 18.20, Sat 15.40, 17.45, Sun and bank hols only 10.15. Journey to the Portela pass approx. 20 mins.

Walk 5

Out: Line 129 (CCSG) Funchal – Camacha via Vale Paraíso, from Funchal Mon–Fri 8.00, 9.00, 10.00, 11.00, 11.45, 12.15, 13.00, 13.30, 14.30, 15.30, Sat 8.15, 9.00, 10.00, 11.00, 11.45, 13.25, 14.35, 15.30, Sun and bank hols 9.00, 10.00, 11.00, 12.30, 13.30, 14.30, 15.30.

Line 77 (CCSG) Funchal – Santo da Serra via Vale Paraíso, from Funchal Mon–Fri 7.35, 10.30, 14.00, Sat 7.40, 10.30, 14.00, Sun 8.30, 10.30, 14.00.

Return: Line 129 (CCSG) Camacha – Funchal via Vale Paraíso, from Camacha Shopping Mon–Fri 10.45, 11.45, 12.30, 13.00, 13.45, 14.15, 15.15, 16.15, 17.40, 18.45, 19.15, 19.45 and 22.45, Sat 10.45, 11.45, 12.30, 13.15–16.15 hourly, 17.45, 19.15, 19.45 and 22.45, Sun and bank hols 10.45, 11.45, 13.15, 14.15, 15.15, 16.15, 17.45, 18.45, 21.00 and 22.45.

Line 77 (CCSG) Santo da Serra – Funchal via Vale Paraíso, from Santo da Serra Mon–Fri 9.00, 12.00, 16.15 and 18.00, Sat 16.15 and 18.00, Sun and bank hols 12.00, 16.15 and 18.00.

Walk 6

Out: Line 36 (Horários do Funchal). Hourly/half-hourly departures from Funchal on Rua Artur Sousa Pinga, east of the Electricity Museum, near valley station of Funchal – Monte cable car. Alight at Campo 1º de Maio.

Line 29 (CCSG) Camacha – Funchal – Camacha. Departures from Camacha and Funchal hourly/half-hourly, less frequent on Sun.

Return: Lines 20 and 21 (Horários do Funchal) into the centre, Line 48 goes to Funchal hotel district. Departs hourly/half-hourly.

Line 22 (Horários do Funchal) from Babosas to the centre. Departs hourly/half-hourly.

Walk 7

Out: Lines 20 and 21 (Horários do Funchal) Funchal – Monte, departs hourly/half-hourly.

Line 22 (Horários do Funchal) Funchal – Babosas, departs hourly/half-hourly.

Walk 8

Out: Line 53 (SAM) Funchal – Faial, from Funchal Mon–Sat 10.00, 13.15.

Line 56 (CCSG) Funchal – Poiso – Faial, from Funchal Mon–Fri 8.10 and 10.00.

Return: From Referta, Line 53 (SAM) Faial – Funchal, from Faial Mon–Fri 13.10, 15.40, 17.15, 18.20, Sat 15.40, 17.45, Sun only 10.15.

From Cruz district, Line 53 (SAM) Faial – Machico – Funchal, from Faial Mon–Fri 13.10, 15.40, 17.15, 18.20, Sat 15.40, 17.45, Sun only 10.15.

Line 56 (CCSG) Santana – Funchal, from Santana Mon–Fri 12.30, 15.30, Sat 12.00, Sun 15.30.

Line 103 (CCSG) Arco de São Jorge – Funchal, from Arco de São Jorge Mon–Fri 12.15, Sat 12.30 and 16.30, Sun 16.30.

Walk 9

Out: Line 53 (SAM) Funchal – Machico – Faial, from Funchal Mon–Sat 10.00, 13.15, from Machico Mon–Fri 9.00, 10.50, 14.10, Sat 10.50.

Line 56 (CCSG) Santana – Funchal, from Funchal Mon–Fri 8.10 and 10.00, Sat 10.00, from Santana Mon–Fri 12.30, Sat 12.00.

Line 103 (CCSG) Funchal – Arco de São Jorge, from Funchal Mon–Sat 7.30 and 13.30, Sun and bank hols 7.30.

Return: Line 53 (SAM) Faial – Machico – Funchal, from Faial Mon–Fri 13.10, 15.40, 17.15, 18.20, Sat 15.40, 17.45, Sun only 10.15.

Line 56 (CCSG) Santana – Funchal, from Santana Mon–Fri 12.30, 15.30, Sat 12.00, Sun 15.30, from Funchal Mon–Fri 17.05.

Line 103 (CCSG) Arco de São Jorge – Funchal, from Arco de São Jorge Mon–Fri 12.15 and 16.30, Sun only 16.30.

Walk 10

Out: Line 56 (CCSG) Funchal – Santana, from Funchal Mon–Fri 8.10, 10.00, Sat 10.00, Sun 10.30, journey approx. 1 hr.

Line 103 (CCSG) Funchal – Arco de São Jorge, from Funchal Mon–Fri 13.30, Sat and Sun 7.30.

Return: Line 53 (SAM) Faial – Funchal, from Faial Mon–Fri 13.10, 15.40, 17.15, 18.20, Sat 15.40, 17.45, Sun only 10.15. Journey from Faial to the Portela pass approx. 15 mins.

Walk 11

Out: Line 103 (CCSG) Funchal – Arco de São Jorge, from Funchal Mon–Fri 13.30, Sat, Sun and bank hols 7.30. Journey to Ribeiro Frio approx. 45 mins.

Line 56 (CCSG) Funchal – Santana, from Funchal Mon–Fri 8.10, 10.00, Sat 10.00, Sun 10.30.

Return: Line 103 (CCSG) Arco de São Jorge – Funchal, from Ribeiro Frio Mon–Fri 18.12, Sat, Sun and bank hols 18.36.

Line 56 (CCSG) Santana – Funchal, from Ribeiro Frio Mon–Fri 13.15 (13.45 in school holidays).

Intercity buses for Madeira hikers

The east of Madeira is served by Sociedade de Automóveis da Madeira, SAM for short, and its green-white-cream coloured buses (timetables at www.sam.pt). The company's central station in Funchal is located on Rua Gulbenkian.

Services in the west are operated by Rodoeste (timetables at www.rodoeste.pt). Central departure points for their red and white buses are located along the Avenida do Mar in Funchal.

Curral das Freiras, Camacha, Santo do Serra and some places on the north coast are served by CCSG (timetables at www.horariosdofunchal.pt, under Carreiras Interurbanas), the Companhia de Carros de São Gonçalo, with their buses painted grey, green and white. They depart from the Avenida do Mar in Funchal.

Walk 12

Out: Line 103 (CCSG) Funchal – Arco de São Jorge, from Funchal Mon–Fri 7.30, 13.30, Sat 7.30, 13.30, Sun 7.30.

Return: Line 103 (CCSG) Arco de São Jorge – Funchal, from Arco de São Jorge Mon–Fri 12.15, 16.30, Sat 12.30 and 16.30, Sun 16.30. Journey to Santana 45–60 mins.

Walk 13

No bus connection.

Walk 14

From ER 101, follow the directions for car drivers.

Out: Line 103 (CCSG) Funchal – Arco de São Jorge, from Funchal Mon–Fri 7.30, 13.30, Sat 7.30, 13.30, Sun 7.30.

Return: Line 103 (CCSG) Arco de São Jorge – Funchal, from Arco de São Jorge Mon–Fri 12.15, 16.30, Sat 12.30, 16.30, Sun 16.30.

Line 138 (CCSG) Funchal – Cabanas, from Funchal Mon–Fri 18.30 and 19.30.

Walk 15

Out: Line 6 (Rodoeste) Funchal – Arco de São Jorge, from Funchal daily at 7.35. Line 6 (Rodoeste) São Vicente – Arco de São Jorge, from São Vicente Mon–Fri 10.00 and 10.45, Sat/Sun/bank hols only 10.00.

Line 103 (CCSG) Funchal – Arco de São Jorge, from Funchal Mon–Sat 7.30, 13.30, Sun 7.30.

Return: Line 6 (Rodoeste) Arco de São Jorge – Funchal, from Arco de São Jorge daily at 14.30, Sun only 17.40.

Line 103 (CCSG) Arco de São Jorge – Funchal, from Arco de São Jorge daily at 16.30.

Walk 16

Out: Line 56 (CCSG) Funchal – Santana, from Funchal Mon–Fri 8.10, 10.00, Sat 10.00, Sun 10.30.

Line 103 (CCSG) Funchal – Arco de São Jorge (via Santana), from Funchal daily at 7.30.

Return: Line 56 (CCSG) Santana – Funchal, from Santana daily (not Sat) at 15.30.

Line 103 (CCSG) Arco de São Jorge – Funchal (via Santana), from Arco de

São Jorge Mon–Sat 12.30, 16.30, Sun 16.30. Journey to Santana 45–60 mins.

Walk 17

No bus connections.

Walk 18

Out: Line 81 (CCSG) Funchal – Curral (via Eira do Serrado), from Funchal Mon–Fri 9.00, 10.00, 11.00, Sat 8.45, 10.00, 11.30, Sun 9.05, 11.40.

Return: Line 81 (CCSG) Curral das Freiras – Funchal (via Eira do Serrado), from Curral (Lombo Chão) Mon–Fri 11.15, 13.40, 14.30, 16.15, Sat 13.15, 14.30, Sun 13.00, 14.30. If you are not returning to Eira do Serrado, there are more return journey options (→ Walk 19: back).

Walk 19

Out: Line 96 (Rodoeste) Funchal – Corticeiras, from Funchal Mon–Fri 8:05, 9.45, 13.20, Sat and Sun 8.05. Stop on the Estrada Municipal do Marco e Fonte da Pedra, give driver Boca dos Namorados as your destination. Or, go to Estreito de Câmara de Lobos and take the taxi from there to Boca dos Namorados. This saves the climb up to Boca dos Namorados.

Line 137 (Rodoeste) Funchal – Estreito de Câmara de Lobos, from Funchal Mon–Fri 8.05, 9.15, 10.10, 11.15, 12.10, 12.40, 13.05, 14.15, Sat 8.00, 10.10, 11.15, 12.10, 13.30, 14.15.

Return: Line 81 (CCSG) Curral das Freiras/Lombo de Chão – Funchal, Mon–Fri 10.15, 11.15, 12.25, 13.40, 14.30, 16.15, 17.55, 19.30, Sat 12.00, 13.15, 14.30, 17.45, Sun 10.30, 13.00, 14.30, 17.35. Bus stop (Rua Eng. Ornelas Camacho) in the upper part of Curral das Freiras at the end of the walk route. Journey from Lombo de Chão to here approx. 10 mins.

Walk 20

Out: Line 81 (CCSG) Funchal – Curral das Freiras (via Fajã dos Cardos), from Funchal Mon–Fri 6.55, 7.35, 8.25, 9.00, 10.00, 11.00 and 12.30, Sat 7.40, 8.45, 10.00 and 11.30, Sun and bank hols 6.40, 9.05 and 11.40.

To collect your car in the evening. Line 81 (CCSG) Funchal – Curral das Freiras (via Fajã dos Cardos), from Funchal Mon–Fri 16.30, 17.00 (not in school holidays), 17.30, 18.10, 18.35, 19.30, 20.30, 21.45 and 23.45, Sat 16.30, 19.30, 23.45, Sun 16.30, 19.30 and 23.45.

Return: Line 6 (Rodoeste) Arco São Jorge – Funchal, from Arco de São Jorge daily at 14.30 (passes the Encumeada pass between 15.30 and 16.00).

Walk 21

Out: Line 96 (Rodoeste) Funchal – Corticeiras/Jardim da Serra, from Funchal Mon–Fri 8.05, 9.45, 12.15. From the terminus, climb approx. 2 km up the steep approach to Boca da Corrida.

Return: Line 81 (CCSG) Curral das Freiras/Lombo Chão – Funchal (via Fajã Escura) from Lombo do Chão Mon–Fri 12.25, Wed 16.15, Sat 13.15, Sun 14.30.

Bus stops on the valley road. Line 81 (CCSG) Curral das Freiras/Lombo Chão (via Fajã dos Cardos) from Lombo do Chão Mon–Fri 12.25, 14.30, 16.15 and 17.55 (17.45 in school holidays), Sat 13.15, 14.30 and 17.45, Sun and bank hols 14.30 and 17.35.

Walks 22, 23, 24, 25 and 26

No bus connections.

Walk 27

Out: Line 127 (Rodoeste) Ribeira Brava – Boa Morte, from Ribeira Brava Mon–Fri 8.00 (with stop at Levada do Norte), 11.10 and 13.20, Sat 8.45, 11.10, Sun only 8.45. From the terminus, walk 10 mins up the street to Snackbar Pinheiro by the waterworks.

Line 148 (Rodoeste) Funchal – Boa Morte Mon–Sat 13.05.

Return: From Cabo Girão to the old regional road ER 229. Here, numerous bus operators operate routes to Ribeira Brava and towards Funchal.

All departure times are only estimates and serve as guides. The summer and winter schedules only differ slightly. To be on the safe side, check the timetables. No buses operate on 25 December.

Walk 28

No reliable bus connection for walkers.

Walk 29

Out: Various connections are available from Ribeira Brava to Ponta do Sol; Ribeira Brava is well connected to Funchal.

Return: Various connections (hourly/half-hourly) from Ribeira Brava to Ponta do Sol and Funchal.

Walk 30

No direct bus connections.

Walk 31

No adequate bus connections.

Walk 32

Out: Line 142 (Rodoeste) Funchal – Raposeira via Ribeira Brava and Estrela da Calheta, from Funchal daily at 8.05, Mon–Fri 12.00.

Return: Line 142 (Rodoeste) Ponta do Pargo – Funchal via Estrela da Calheta and Ribeira Brava, from Ponta do Pargo daily at 14.30.

Line 80 (Rodoeste) Porto Moniz – Funchal via Estrela da Calheta and Ribeira Brava, from Porto Moniz daily at 16.00. Journey to Ponta do Pargo 45 mins.

From Restaurant A Carreta to Ponta do Pargo 13.45, 14.30 and 15.30.

Walks 33, 34 and 35

No bus connections.

Walk 36

Out: Line 6 (Rodoeste) Funchal – Arco de São Jorge, from Funchal daily at 7.35; Arco de São Jorge – Funchal from São Vicente 7.45. Journey from Funchal to Encumeada pass approx. 2–2.15 hrs. From São Vicente to Encumeada pass 30 mins.

Return: Line 6 (Rodoeste) Arco de São Jorge – Funchal, from São Vicente approx. 15.30.

Walk 37

No bus connection.

► Websites for hikers

www.visitmadeira.pt: Official site of the Madeira tourist board. Includes notes on walking trails and their accessibility.

www.madeira-levada-walks.com: Site of Madeira Explorers walking tours. Guided walks with local guides; many years of experience.

www.pnm.pt: Website of the Parque Natural da Madeira, also in English.

www.madeiraislandnews.com: News blog, also active on Facebook.

www.procivmadeira.pt: Madeira Civil Protection Service site with information on closed streets and paths (also in English).

www.madeira-seekers.com: General tour agency. Tourist information, car hire and hiking tours. ■

► Maps: There are several general maps covering the island that are easily available.

The maps in this book should be sufficient for the hiking routes – however, they show only the area around each walk. The best walking map to the whole island is *Madeira F&B 1:30,000* (£9.99), published by Freytag-Berndt at a scale of 1:30,000. A military map of Madeira at 1:25,000 scale has been produced in nine sheets by the Instituto Geográfico do Exército (www.igeoe.pt), though it is not clear whether all the paths shown are still accessible. These can be bought direct online and are also found in some bookshops in Funchal, though all nine sheets are rarely available. ■

► Books

Top 10 Madeira. DK Eyewitness Travel, £8.99, 128pp, 2018. Overview travel guide covering the whole island. There are similar guides from several other publishers: Lonely Planet, Marco Polo, Insight and Berlitz.

For more detail there's *Madeira Marco Polo Travel Handbook*, Marco Polo, £12.99, 244pp, 2015.

Madeira – A Botanical Melting Pot! Susanne Lipps, Oliver Breda Verlag, €12.95, 2016, is a flora guide published by the author of this book.

For natural history there's *Madeira's Natural History in a Nutshell*, Peter Sziemer, Francisco Ribeiro & Filhos, 2000. Only available on Madeira, but worth seeking out. Available from mid-2018, look out for *Wildlife of Madeira & The Canary Islands: A Photographic Field Guide*, John Bowler, Princeton University Press, £19.95, 224pp, 2018.

The Madeira Story Centre in Funchal sells a small yet interesting brochure on the history of Madeira: *Madeira – A Short Illustrated History*.■

Climb to São Jorge (Walk 12)

** Along Ponta de São Lourenço, Madeira's eastern tip

Although the eastern tip of Madeira is actually its driest part, the hike from Baía da Abra bay over the island's most easterly peak, Ponta do Furado, and the subsequent descent to the sea at the Cais do Sardinha jetty, is exceptionally varied and also suitable for children. Where else can you find alpine terrain so close to sea level?

▶▶ The route starts at the end of the street, by the large car park **1** and bus stop, beside the **Baía da Abra**. A signpost points the way towards Cais do Sardinha. A short distance along a wide gravel path, the route descends to the right, down long, wide steps. The next stage of the route, a boardwalk, then comes into view. A wooden bridge spans a dry valley, before the boardwalk ascends gently with a short set of steps. After a few metres, the wooden surface ends and the path continues on stony ground.

A long bend to the left provides a delightful view of the ridges of the Ponta do Furado, Madeira's easternmost peak, to the right. A large rock arch sits in the Atlantic at the foot. The outline of the mountain resembles a giant elephant's head. Gilthead sea bream are farmed offshore in pools in the bay. Straight after the long left-hand bend, a weather-worn stone wall cuts across the hillside. Before the Ponta de São Lourenço was declared a nature reserve, such walls used to house herds of goats. Today, the area is a 'Zona de Recuperação de Flora'. This designation aims to protect the sparse, sensitive coastal vegetation and hikers should not leave the path.

The route continues on a path made safe by wire cables. Steps, some of which are cut into the rock, lead down to a wayside cross. From here, you can enjoy the wonderful vista of the island's north coast. The

View of the peaks of the Ponta do Furado

path continues down and to the right, ending at a shingle beach. A spectacular viewpoint **2** can be found only a few steps to the left. The Atlantic Ocean, churned up by the north-east trade wind, surrounds the striking rocks; swathes of ochre and red with tones of brown, black and beige create a desert-like aspect. From this viewpoint, the route goes back to the crossroads and then to the left, up some steps and along a wire cable railing.

After a short climb, the path takes a sharp left **3** and leads up red steps cut into the red tuff hillside (→ p. 12). Continue up this gentle incline and onto stony ground until you reach steps with wire cable railings **4** leading downhill. After only a few steps, the path comes to a sort of saddle. From here, you can enjoy views of more fascinating rock formations.

The well-secured trail then continues along the hillside, remaining level for most of the time. After crossing this hillside, the path takes a slight left turn and rises gently, where it cuts across another hillside. To the right, in the distance, the view extends to the pillars that support the airport runway. Along with the bridge over the River Tagus in Lisbon, the runway is considered one of Portugal's architectural master-pieces.

After this slope, the path reaches an exposed point **5** with magnificent views of the waters below. This point is also very well protected, helping to keep any feelings of dizziness in check.

Relatively steep rocky steps then lead you down a narrow ridge. This passage is only a few metres long, with railings to the left and right.

After the ridge, the path continues down rocky ground and, after a slight left turn, reaches another viewpoint **6** with views of a tuff rock face (→ p. 12) cut through with veins of trachyte and basalt. ▶

Length/walking time: return distance approx. 7.2 km, total of 3 hrs inclusive summit of Ponta do Furado.

Terrain: the ground is rocky and sandy in places; some sections require **sure-footedness.** Elevated sections are well protected with wire cable railings. In strong winds, it is best to forgo the summit of the Ponta do Furado.

Feature: at Cais do Sardinha **10** you can bathe in the calm sea – however, no shower or toilet facilities are available.

Marking: none, but the path is quite clear.

Equipment: wind and sun protection! The sun's rays are powerful even under cloud cover. Pack a bathing suit and shoes or trekking sandals as you wish. Sturdy, ankle-high walking shoes are advisable.

Supplies: be sure to take plenty of drinking water, as the sun and wind are extremely dehydrating. A mobile kiosk can usually be found early in the afternoon at the car park **1** by Baía da Abra, selling ice creams and cold drinks – but don't rely on it!

Getting there: if driving by car, drive to the end of the Machico – Caniçal motorway and follow signs for 'Ponta de São Lourenço'. The large car park is at the end of the street. Bus → p. 26.

Walk 1

View of the volcanic landscape

▶ The path is largely level as it crosses another hillside. A left-hand bend **7** then leads the path away from the Cais do Sardinha. However, the route follows this left-hand bend and, a little later, passes to the left of the **Casa do Sardinha**. The small, stone-built house is surrounded by palm trees. It belongs to the nature reserve management and, sadly, is no longer manned, but does house a small exhibition on the nature of Madeira's eastern tip. The shade beside the house is the perfect spot for a break. (Due to the shortage of water, use of toilet facilities is charged at €1.)

After passing the house, a path forks **8** off towards the peaks of the eastern tip. The climb is not particularly difficult, though the descent is rather slippery. 10 minutes later, the well maintained path comes to a pre-summit, after which it reaches a small saddle – a short stretch where **sure-footedness and a head for heights are absolutely necessary** – before continuing up to the second summit **9**. You then turn

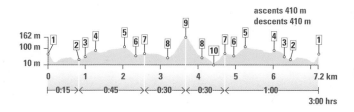

around and follow the same path back to the fork **8**.

From the peaks, follow the path straight down to the **Cais do Sardinha 10**, which is actually nothing more than a set of concrete steps down to the Atlantic where nature reserve wardens moor their boats. In calm seas, you can bathe in the clear waters or relax on the adjacent shingle beach. Directly above the Cais do Sardinha, a wooden bridge leads over a narrow, shallow dry valley to an area surrounded by natural stone walls. The path continues straight through to the other side, ascending gradually with handrails for safety.

After a short climb, you reach the familiar path **7** and follow it back to the car park **1**. ■

The rocky coastal landscape

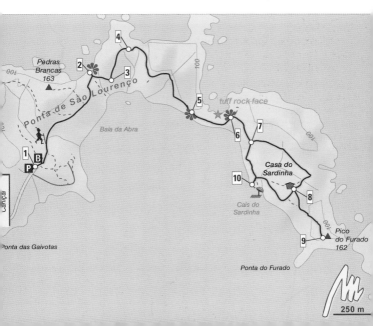

* From Maroços to the old Caniçal tunnel

Easy levada-based walk with glimpses into rural life and an enjoyable detour to the Boca do Risco viewpoint.

▶▶ Opposite the Bar Calçadinha in Maroços is the starting point  **1** of this levada walk, where a metal sign ('Caniçal') shows the way. The water channel is not immediately obvious, as this section is covered, but the typically level route is unmistakeable. After a short distance, the path passes a junction with narrow roads, but you should continue to follow the flat route past several houses.

The levada is then uncovered as it runs along small field terraces. A steep road **2** must be crossed diagonally to the left; a concrete ramp then leads back down to the levada. The channel then passes into a steep, meticulously terraced valley where pineapples, avocados, sugar cane, maize and Japanese medlars (also known as loquats) are grown.

The subsequent valleys also feature intensive farming, with the laborious work on the steep slopes undertaken by hand. After passing through several ravines, the route crosses an old cobbled path **3** lined with street lights so that locals can use it at night (the path only leads

A picturesque setting: houses by the levada

Art in a vegetable garden

to fields). A little further along, the path leads through a 35 m long tunnel, but a torch is not necessary.

Beyond the tunnel, the levada runs along a steep rock face, however the path is wide. At a waterhouse **4** dating from 1954, a narrow levada branches off away from your path to the right. Beyond the waterhouse, continue along the level Levada do Caniçal into a wide valley. In the last valley branch, the valley floor is traversed by a concrete crossing **5** before the path leads out of the valley and Bar O Jacaré **6** to the left invites you to take a breather, with tables and chairs right beside the levada path.

A few minutes' walk on from the bar, the levada bends to the left into another wide valley. After the main channel of the valley, look out for a cobbled path **7** ▶

Length/walking time: approx. 13.4 km, 4:05 hrs (incl. 1 hr for the detour to Boca do Risco and back to the levada).

Terrain: easy yet varied long-distance walk through cultivated land. Sure-footedness is only needed for the detour to Boca do Risco.

Marking: none, but the route along the levada is obvious.

Equipment: sturdy walking shoes.

Supplies: take water. Bar Calçadinha at the start **1**. Bar O Jacaré **6** serves snacks every day. Bar Levada Nova on the road to Machico, 9am–9pm daily, ☏ 291-617505.

Getting there: take the car from Machico along the Via Expresso towards Porto da Cruz/Santana to the exit for Maroços/Portela. The levada starts on the right directly after the exit. Taxi rank in Machico ☏ 291-962480. Bus → p. 26.

Walk 2

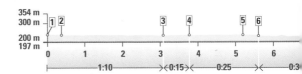

►that comes up to meet the levada from the right and continues upwards to the left over natural stone steps. The section to the right has street lights almost up to the levada; a small house sits below the levada to the right.

This path is the start of the **detour to the Boca do Risco pass**: climb the steps to the left and walk along a weathered natural stone wall where the surface is well worn and the path, which has narrowed over time, leads over crags in places. Various narrow paths break away from the main route, but only lead to fields of crops. Your path runs below a field terrace with corrugated sheet metal walls **8** and swings to the left up to the pass. After negotiating a further short climb, you reach the **Boca do Risco** pass **9**. By walking just a few steps further, you reach the north side of the island with magnificent views of the coastal cliffs. (The famous north coast path starts at the Boca do Risco pass. It

Many hillsides have been laboriously terraced

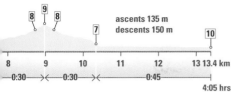

ascents 135 m
descents 150 m

| 8 | 9 | 10 | 11 | 12 | 13 13.4 km |

— 0:30 —><— 0:30 —><— 0:45 —

4:05 hrs

was restored and made safe in 2016, but continues to suffer from land-slides. The path requires a head for heights but, if in good condition, offers splendid views.)

Then, follow the same path from the Boca do Risco pass back to the levada and the junction with the cobbled path **7**. In dry conditions, the descent is negotiated faster than the ascent, but in wet conditions the opposite may be true. When you reach the levada, bear left and continue on the level path. After a few valleys, the Pico do Facho with its transmission masts and the old road from Machico to Caniçal (regional road ER 214) come into view. The path first crosses a new road, and then continues past several houses until it reaches the picturesque house of a levada warden **10**.

Turn right onto the road and after 30 m, on the right is the first bus stop. (To the left, the path continues through the old Caniçal tunnel to the former whaling town of Caniçal). However, follow the road to the right along a long lefthand bend and, after about 5 mins, you reach the Bar Levada Nova. Buses stop diagonally opposite – but only on request! ∎

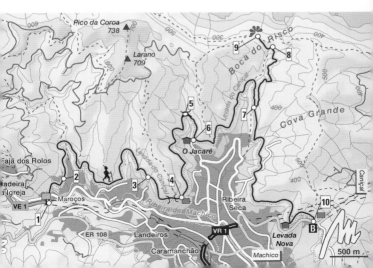

✳✳ Through the laurel forest over the Portela pass

From the Portela pass, the route first heads to the Casa das Funduras lodge, and then carries on via Fajã dos Rolos to a viewpoint with a scenic picnic spot, and then through Ribeira de Machico and back to the Portela pass. The laurel forest(→ p. 16), which this route cuts through, is a special feature of international importance due to its low altitude; it was designated a UNESCO World Heritage Site in 1999.

Alternative

Take ER 101 by car to Ribeira de Machico (park on the road to Fajã dos Rolos near the ER 108). Take bus 20 or 53 from there to the Portela pass (bus stop located directly after junction towards Fajã dos Rolos). This saves the final climb of about 30 minutes up a narrow road.

▶▶ The starting point is the **Portela pass** 🔳. To the left of the 'Miradouro da Portela' restaurant, a narrow road leads north-east. Wooden signs are located along the road ('P. R. 5 Maroços 8 km', 'PBTT Joel Funduras 7.1 km', 'Fajã dos Rolos 12.8 km') – for practical reasons, the route described here is a combination of these paths. A little further down the road is an information board with details of the various walking routes. Further on, at an intersection 🔳 in a right-hand bend, bear left.

Fabulous vista towards Eagle Rock on the north coast

After about 10 m, the road becomes a forest trail. Where the tarmac stops, a narrow path branches off to the left (marked with 'Caminho Municipal Portela Cruz da Guarda'), but your route instead heads straight on to a second information board and then continues on the broad forest track.

A subsequent right-hand curve **3** provides a lovely view of the striking **Eagle Rock (Penha de Águia)**, which looms over Porto da Cruz. A few steps further, the path passes a deep, narrow tunnel with no exit. The levada, which has been running to the right of the wide path almost from the start, flows past this before disappearing into another tunnel **4** a few steps later. The forest trail leads you to the left of this tunnel and, after a large bend in the forest track, meets the levada once again. About 80 m further on, the track forks **5**: bear left here and follow the path just below the levada (signposts for 'Funduras' and 'Fajã dos Rolos'.)

Directly after the fork, the path is lined to the left by fine specimens of the lily-of-the-valley tree (Clethra arborea) (→ p. 18), which flowers in July. Further on, look out for a narrow path branching off into the forest to the right. A picturesque wooden railing made from tree heath and a wooden sign with the inscription 'Serra das Funduras Percurso Pedonal D. R. F.' mark the start of this path **6**. At this point, leave the track and bear right along the narrow but distinct path through the laurel forest. The forest is interspersed with tree heath and bog myrtle.

The path continues through the dense, shaded forest with gentle inclines and descents but no significant changes in altitude. At a clearing **7**, the path can be overgrown with brambles at certain times of year if it has not been recently maintained. However, this section is very short, and the path then leads back into the dark forest and reaches a short set of soil steps leading up to the track, which you should then follow down to the right. A few minutes later, the track curves sharply to the right **8**; at   its ▶

Length/walking time: approx. 14.7 km, 5:10 hrs.

Terrain: easy circular walk on wide forest tracks and narrow but safe paths through the laurel forest; sometimes runs along small, quiet roads.

Marking: none; signs and overview maps at some points.

Equipment: sturdy walking shoes. Sun and rain protection. Jumpers and wind jackets are also advisable in the laurel forest.

Supplies: take drinking water! Bar-Restaurante Miradouro da Portela at the pass **1**, daily from noon, ✆ 291-966169; Bar-Restaurante Portela à Vista, daily from noon, ✆ 291-963189, a few metres down from the pass on the ER 101 to Machico. Bar O Caniçal **21** in Fajã dos Rolos, open daily – you may need to knock or shout, ✆ 291-963925. Some bars in Ribeira de Machico.

Getting there: by car, take the ER 101 to the Portela pass or the ER 102 via Santo da Serra. Parking available at Restaurant Miradouro da Portela. Taxi rank in Machico ✆ 291-962480, ✆ 291-9621989, ✆ 291-9622220 or ✆ 291-552100 in Santo (António) da Serra. Bus → p. 26.

Walk 3

▶ apex, the walking trail branches off to the left. Steps cut into the earth lead into the forest and past a picnic spot with a table and benches.

At first, the forest is not particularly dense, as cluster pines are intertwined with the laurel trees – yet more primeval, earthy sections await just a little further on. After some climbs and descents, the path reaches another forest trail directly beside the **Casa das Funduras** lodge **9** and picnic tables.

In front of the Casa das Funduras, the path continues to the left on the virtually flat forest trail. After about 2 minutes, a path joins from the right, but this can be ignored: continue up the main track, which then curves to the left. After the curve, earthen steps again lead down to the narrow forest path **10** – the start of this path is obvious, and a wooden railing is a key marker. Although the path doesn't start in the best condition, it improves as you walk further.

Steps in the earth **11** unexpectedly lead uphill – depending on the time of year, these may not be obvious. Though the path does continue straight ahead, turn left and go up these steps. After a short yet steep ascent, you rejoin the track and reach a picnic area **12** with a lovely view of Machico and the **Pico do Facho** to the left above the bay of Machico.

The forest track then climbs even higher, but this picnic area is the start of the return journey. This forest trail leads downhill, and the scent of the laurel forest returns.

This wide track soon reaches the Casa das Funduras **9** and continues past it and upwards to a fork in the path **13** with several signposts. Take the path down to the left towards Fajã dos Rolos (signposted).

Ignore a path branching off to the left **14** some 5 minutes later. Continue down the path, ignore another one branching off to the left in a right-hand bend **15** (as it leads to

Maroços) and head down the path to the right. The laurel forest becomes increasingly permeated by eucalyptus trees, and although a North American cypress species had once developed a considerable forest on some slopes, many of these trees have since fallen victim to storms. The original vegetation of the laurel forest managed to survive in narrow side valleys and on the steep rock faces.

The route then sweeps around various valleys: in the floor of one narrow valley, the laurel forest can again be seen thriving. Beyond it, the route bends sharply to the left and, after the apex **16**, gently ascends out of the valley. The laurel forest also dominates the following valley. Further on, the path reaches a signposted fork **17**, where another forest path descends to join from the right. Take a slight left turn, continuing more or less straight on. The next stage of the route is marked by a signpost to Fajã dos Rolos. ▶

▶ Another forest path then joins from the left **18**, and can be ignored; a short while later, the path approaches an isolated house **19**. A further forest path joins from the left before the path reaches another house,

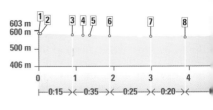

this time belonging to Fajã dos Rolos. A board directly in front of the house provides information on local paths and trails.

The route then continues along a level road, and a short stretch later the surface turns into tarmac. A steep, concrete road branches off and down to the left, but your route follows the flatter road to the right. At what seems like a turning area, the road curves to the right, and the walk continues along this street and through Fajã dos Rolos. If you're in need of light refreshment, the Bar O Caniçal **20** is located on the left-hand side of the street.

The road then continues to the next small village, **Ribeira de Machico**, and passes by a church immediately followed by a road intersection with a stop sign; there are signposts for Machico to the left and Portela to the right.

Madeira's laurel forest – a World Heritage Site

The evergreen laurel forests are a special characteristic of the subtropic climate zone in the northern hemisphere: in the EU, such extensive laurel populations are only found on Madeira, the Azores and the Canary Islands. Heavy rainfall in the warm summer months and barely any frost in the humid but mild winter are ideal conditions for the laurel species that dominate these unique forests (you can see the four main species of this genus here on p. 13). This humid trade wind zone in the North Atlantic provides the basic climatic conditions: the rising northeasterly winds condense on the island's slopes and supply the necessary moisture. On Madeira, this zone on the north side of the island typically lies between 600–1300 m above sea level. On the south side, such vegetation only grows at higher elevations reached by fog. The forest to the west of the Portela pass is therefore particularly remarkable, and is also the largest contiguous laurel forest on the southern side of the island.

UNESCO designated this laurel forest a World Heritage Site in 1999. It is also part of the 'Natura 2000 Network' (http://ec.europa.eu/environment/nature), a network of protected areas that spans the entire EU with the stated goal of retaining biodiversity. In addition, the laurel forest is of fundamental importance to the island's water balance. Although Madeira does not suffer from a lack of rainfall, the steep terrain means that rain flows (too) quickly into the ocean. While 10 % of the rain that falls on the laurel forest becomes groundwater, only 1% of the rain that falls on built-up land or the eucalyptus forest also follows the same path. The rest quickly disappears into streams, rivers and the sewage system. Thanks to its vast water retention capacity, the laurel forest protects the island from erosion in a way no other form of vegetation is able to do.

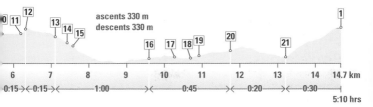

ascents 330 m
descents 330 m

Turn right and, about 3 minutes later, the road reaches a round-about **21**. To complete the route, follow the sign to the Portela pass and walk along this road for about 30 minutes and almost 2 km back up to the starting point **1**.

Alternatively, turn left at the roundabout **21** to reach the old regional road ER 108 (cf. map), which leads from Machico and over the Portela pass. Immediately on the right is a bus stop for services towards Portela, while the stop on the opposite side of the road is for services in the direction of Machico. ■

In the laurel forest

* Along the Levada da Serra do Faial to the Portela pass

If you love woodland landscapes this easy Levada walk is for you. It takes you from Sítio das Quatro Estradas through wild laurel forest.

▶▶ The starting point **1** is on regional road ER 202 from Santo da Serra to the Poiso pass above a former pig farm. At the entrance to the levada, signposts point toward Camacha to the west and Portela, the destination of this route, to the east. A broad meadow path runs along the levada, starting above the derelict former pig farm.

The walk begins in a eucalyptus forest, though other trees such as old gnarled oaks, pines and a few laurels start to appear after about 15 minutes. A wide track **2** then crosses the path, but your level route continues and follows a left-hand bend, passing a levada warden's house immediately after the bend.

You then walk through an idyllic side valley filled with laurel trees, before crossing an old natural stone bridge **3** leading over the valley floor. Another old bridge then appears. After this second bridge, a wide path descends from the left to meet yours: don't take it. The vegetation becomes wilder and more interesting and includes tree heath, occasional specimens of the endemic Madeira blueberry (→ p. 18), knotted old oaks covered with ferns and other typical laurel forest flora. Beard lichen on the trees attest to the high air humidity and good air quality.

Once again – this time from below – a wide path joins yours **4**, as does another 10 m further on, before a section of the route with relatively monotonous eucalyptus forest follows. This, however, soon gives way to dense vegetation.

After crossing a wide dirt road **5**, the path briefly runs along the narrow levada wall before widening once again. Another path joins ours as we follow a left-hand bend.

Further along the levada, the route passes a waterhouse **6** dating from 1906 that is reminiscent of a prison tower. The Japanese cedars

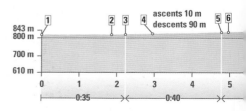

in this area are particularly striking. Signposts have been attached to the corner of the building (e.g. you could follow the path down to Santo da Serra), but your route leads further along the levada towards Portela.

About 10 minutes after the waterhouse, your route branches off onto a narrow path **7** leading down to the right and enables you to bypass a narrow, slippery section along the levada wall. This path runs parallel to the levada, slightly below it, and rejoins the levada again **8** before the wide path continues through dark forest.

The path then crosses another wide road **9** before the levada curves once again, with the path becoming narrow and slippery. This section can also be avoided by quickly crossing a small valley and climbing to meet the levada once again on the other side.

You then abruptly reach a stony path **10** leading down to the right with signs for 'Portela'. (There are also signs for Pico do Suna to the left. The detour to the once panoramic mountain is not worthwhile: over time, the trees have grown so tall that nothing but tree trunks can be seen. Straight on, the path leads to Ribeiro Frio and the path of Walk 10; → p. 72. If you head straight on by mistake, you will reach a second waterhouse that also resembles a prison tower. At this point, you've gone too far – and have reached the three-star Route 10.)

The descent may be slippery in wet conditions. After a few minutes, a steep, narrow levada joins the path from the left as you descend. A few steps further down, the path comes to a rather inconspicuous fork **11**: the wide path to the right leads into the forest, while to the left the path ascends with the levada. The latter is more scenic, but the paths join each other before long. Along the narrow levada, steps then lead to the beautifully landscaped park of the ▶

Length/walking time: approx. 9.6 km, 2:40 hrs
Terrain: easy levada-based route; slippery in parts.
Marking: none; occasional signs.
Equipment: sturdy walking shoes.
Supplies: take drinking water; stop for a bite at the Portela pass **16**: Bar/Restaurante Miradouro da Portela, or just below in the Portela à Vista.
Getting there: by car, take the ER 102 between Camacha and Santo António da Serra (often simply called Santo da Serra) to Sítio das 4 Estradas. From here, the ER 202 branches off to the Poiso pass, and after about 600 m passes a large pig farm. The levada runs right above it. There is limited parking space directly by the levada on the roadside, but the grass verge opposite offers plenty of space. Bus → p. 26.
Getting back: by (bus → p. 26) or taxi back to the start, about €12; in Santana ✆ 291-572540, in Machico ✆ 291-962480.

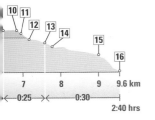

Walk 4

▶ **Lamaceiros forest lodge** 🔢. The trail previously crossed by the levada then joins from the right.

The route cuts straight across the garden area and passes the lodge along a wide road, after which a newly-built reservoir can be seen to the right of the path. A little later, the road reaches a lovely viewpoint 🔢 looking out towards the distinctive **Eagle Rock** (Penha de Águia, → Route 9).

Then, continue downwards on the wide dirt road up to a fork 🔢 in a long right-hand bend close to a large, enclosed area used for agriculture. At this fork, your route leaves the wide road and bears left (following signs for 'Portela') on a path that leads past the enclosed area.

A short, gentle uphill section then follows. At a right-hand bend, a newly-built concrete levada runs alongside the path, which in this section can be very slippery in wet conditions. Follow this path to a short set of steps 🔢 cut into the earth leading down to the left, where the route encounters the remains of a former levada house. Follow these onto a dirt path permeated by tree roots and rocks. It ends at the road from the Portela pass to Santo da Serra.

Follow this road a short distance down to the left to reach the **Portela pass** 🔢. Directly at the pass is the Bar-Restaurante Mira-

Along the levada

douro da Portela; the Bar-Restaurante Portela à Vista is a few metres further down towards Machico. ∎

* From Vale Paraíso to Camacha

The route runs along easy trails through secluded forests and valleys to the basket-weaving village of Camacha.

▶▶ The starting point **1** is on the Levada da Serra do Faial at the point where it crosses the ER 203 to the Poiso pass. The entrance is marked by a tile picture with the inscription 'Levada da Serra do Faial' and a wooden sign pointing towards Santo da Serra. A wide path runs along the levada, which you follow to the east through mixed woodland interspersed with chestnut trees. Following a level path, your route ignores various other trails.

> **Tip**
>
> In Camacha 7, a visit to the basket weaving centre in Café Relógio is worth the trip: in the cellar, visitors can watch the artisans at work.

After circumnavigating a first valley, the path crosses the Caminho Ribeira Grande and continues into the forest. African lilies line the levada, and bella-donna lilies sometimes flower here in autumn. As the route continues, the vegetation alternates between mixed woodland and eucalyptus forest; old oak trees also border the levada path, which for a long time served as a vital connecting route. About 30 minutes from the start, the path crosses the Caminho da Madeira **2** – a tarmac road, where

Fruit and vegetable allotments beside the levada

There are not many signs on this walk but it's easy to follow.

there are more signs for Camacha and Santo da Serra. The path soon comes to the first houses in Achandinha, a district of Camacha. However, before reaching the centre of the village, the levada runs through an idyllic valley and a further side valley.

In **Achadinha**, the path beside the levada is made of concrete. After these houses, leave the channel via some steps **3** that lead down to the left and end at a village road, which you follow up to the left.

Cross the Caminho Municipal da Achadinha, where signs again show the way. This is also the location of the popular Snackbar Moisés **4**. Take a break here if you wish, and then continue on the same road: the levada runs to the left alongside the narrow village road.

After passing two tall transmission masts and the last houses in Achadinha, you reach another pleasant forest trail.

This leads you around a valley with fruit trees and eventually to Igreja, another district of Camacha.

In **Igreja**, the trail is again made from cement and meets a steep road **5** called Caminho Municipal da Portela. Here, the route ascends to the right. Walk over a crest ▶

Length/walking time: approx. 5.2 km, 1:30 hrs.
Terrain: easy levada walk on pleasant paths.
Marking: none; infrequent signs.
Equipment: light walking gear, in wet conditions some sections may be slippery.
Supplies: take water. Snackbar Moisés 4, popular destination, ✆ 961-475461 (mobile); Café Relógio at 7 always open in the daytime.
Getting there: the route can be reached fairly easily from Funchal. Timetables → p. 26. Parking for cars is available by the ER 203. Taxi from Camacha back to the start costs about €5–10.

Walk 5

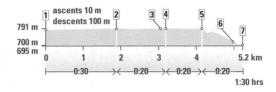

► with large, round water containers and further views into the valley. Follow this road downhill for about 15 minutes until it comes to a junction **6** with another road. Here, bear right and continue past Camacha parish church with its picturesque pavilion.

At the next fork, keep left to reach the **main square 7 of Camacha**, which includes a taxi stand and, on the right-hand (west) side, the bus stop for journeys to Funchal or back to the starting point. Café Relógio is located on the south side of the square. ■

Levada da Serra do Faial

∗ Along the Levada dos Tornos to Monte

This route along one of the island's largest levadas lead from the ER 102 at Palheiro Ferreiro through cultivated land, interspersed with native vegetation in the narrow valleys, to Curral dos Romeiros. The final stretch follows an undulating old cobbled path to Monte.

▶▶ The starting point is on regional road ER 102 **1** from Funchal to Camacha. About 400 m after the turnoff towards Terreiro da Luta, the levada **2** crosses the road, signposted with 'Levada dos Tornos' and 'Monte'. The route continues to the west against the flow of the levada along a wide, gentle path. Paths branching off are ignored, and the route runs continuously alongside the levada as far as Curral dos Romeiros.

Variants

If you prefer to avoid the climbs and descents to Monte, end the walk in Curral dos Romeiros (return with bus 29, min. 1x per hour).

Descent to Funchal from 11 → Walk 7 from 4 (→ p. 58).

At first, the levada cuts through a populated area, but soon curves into a wooded valley filled with aromatic acacias, mocanos, chestnut trees and some isolated Madeira mahogany trees (→ p. 17). Fruit trees also grow near the houses.

After about 20 minutes, some dirt steps **3** descend towards the now unfortunately closed Jasmin Tea House; your route continues to follow the levada. It then continues

Levada warden house at waypoint 6

above the road to Terreiro de Luta, which it soon crosses **4**. A little later, the path passes a poultry farm. The smell is far from pleasant, but at least this section is thankfully only brief.

Further on, the Hortensia Tea House **5** invites you to take a break, and features a well-maintained, artfully-arranged garden. The levada runs around it and then crosses a narrow access route which provides the second entrance to the tea house.

A few minutes later, the levada runs beneath a road. The channel is covered with stepping stones for this section, and for 10 m the path moves through an underpass before leading into a deep valley. At first, the path is lined by tall thujas. After looping round several valley branches, the path crosses a road and, a few steps further, passes a large water basin and a canal maintenance station at an idyllic levada warden house **6**.

Later on, the levada runs by the fence of the old Quinta do Pomar estate, and the path crosses another steep road **7** and then passes close to the terrace of a private residence.

The land behind the following fence **8** belongs to the Hotel Choupana Hills (closed). As levadas must remain accessible at all times, the gate is left open. Only at the second gate do the apartment buildings of the 5 star luxury hotel and health resort become visible to the left and right of the levada. A sign informs walkers that they are entering private property and must not leave the levada path. However, the path crosses the hotel land quickly, with another fence marking the boundary.

The houses visible on the opposite hillside are part of the village of Curral dos Romeiros. However, the levada first leads through a wild and romantic valley in a dark forest.

Three side valleys must be crossed via water overflows; ▶

Length/walking time: approx. 8.7 km, 2:20 hrs.

Terrain: easy levada-based route; the final section along the cobbled path can be slippery in wet conditions.

Marking: none; occasional signs.

Equipment: non-slip shoes.

Supplies: take drinking water. Stop for a bite after 30 minutes at the Hortensia Tea House ⑤ (daily 10am–5pm, ☎ 291-795219, home-made waffles and hearty snacks); towards the end of the route: in the cafeteria by the ticket desk of the Monte – Jardim Botâncio cable car station, in the café by the cable car summit station to Funchal or in the bars by the Largo da Fonte.

Getting there: by car, take the ER 102 from Funchal to Camacha (exit for 'Palheiro Ferreiro/Palheiro Golf'. 400 m after the turnoff to Terreiro da Luta, the Levada dos Tornos crosses the ER 102. Parking available directly by the levada on a small side street.

Bus → p. 26.

Monte – Funchal cable car runs continuously from 9.30am–5.45pm.

Tip: for drivers, it's also a good idea to start the route in Funchal so that, after the walk, you need only take public transport to Funchal and can then drive onwards from there. Almirante Reis car park in Funchal is south of the market hall (signposted).

Walk 6

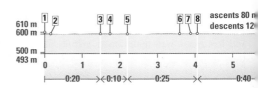

▶ during the wetter season, water can flow here and the ground may therefore become slippery.

Eventually, you reach the first houses of **Curral dos Romeiros**, as some steps **9** lead away from the levada path and down to the left. A red dot and a small red arrow can be seen on a wall here. Your route continues to the right along the old cobbled path where, after a few strides, a sign on the corner of a house points towards the Levada do Bom Sucesso and Monte. You continue along the old cobbled path and ignore a path branching off to the right.

The cobbled path ends at a tarmacked square, and the access road from the left leads into the village. This turning place **10** is the bus 29 terminal for the route between Funchal and Curral dos Romeiros.

Cross straight over this square and continue along a flat stretch of tarmac before a steep descent to a further turning area. The tarmac ends here, and the old cobbled street lined by streetlights then continues.

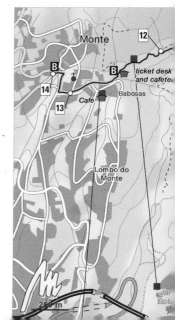

This path starts off relatively even, but steepens increasingly into the Ribeira de João Gomes valley. In a sharp right-hand bend, a narrow path **11** branches off to the left. (If you wish to walk the descent to Funchal, follow the description in Route 7 from **4**, signs point to the Levada do Bom Sucesso leading to Funchal.) Walkers continuing to Monte should stay on the cobbled path which leads across the valley floor over a wide natural stone bridge.

On the other side, the cobbled path climbs again. At the subsequent

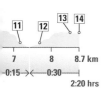

junction **12**, keep left and continue along the cobbled path as it leads below the Monte – Jardim Botânico cable car station. There is a short climb to negotiate in order to reach the ticket desk. Directly beyond it is the Largo das Babosas square, which is the final stop for bus 22. Follow the even, cobbled street and, a few steps later, you reach the summit station of the Monte – Funchal cable car. Just beside it is the entrance to the **Jardim Tropical Monte Palace**.

The cobbled street leads above the garden and on to the start of the wicker toboggan run **13**. However, you should not follow this street used for tobogganing, and instead take a half-right turn at the small toilet cabin onto a path paved with round pebbles that leads to the main square of Largo da Fonte. Cross this square to the left, and you reach the ER 103, the road from Funchal to Poiso. This is the location of the bus stop **14** for services in the direction of Funchal. ■

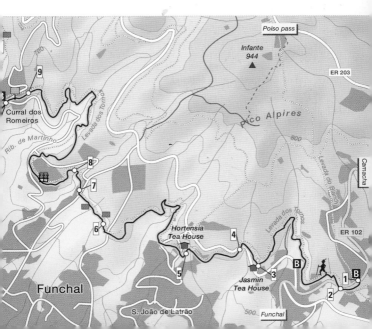

*** From Monte down to Funchal

Note – This path is currently closed. Contact the Posto de Turismo in Funchal (p24) to check reopening date.

Strenuous descent in the isolated valley of Ribeira de Gomes, followed by a short adventure along the Levada do Bom Sucesso – and all in easy reach of the city of Funchal.

▶▶ The route starts at the **summit station** of the Funchal – Monte cable car. (If taking bus lines 20 and 21, you arrive at Largo da Fonte in Monte and should then follow signs for 'teleférico', which lead you to the summit station in a few minutes; if you take bus line 22, start at Largo das Babosas – see below)

From the exit **1** of the Funchal – Monte cable car, the route starts along a cobbled street to the right towards 'teleférico Jardim Botânico'

> **Shortened**
>
> The walk can also be ended on reaching the first street in Funchal **10**. Various bus services stop here, and all go to the coast road in Funchal.

(signposted) that leads to a square with bus stops. Unfortunately, its name, **Largo das Babosas**, is not clearly marked.

On the opposite side is the ticket desk of the Monte – Jardim Botânico cable car. With this on your right, begin to walk downhill.

This newly paved path passes by the terminal of the Jardim Botânico – Monte cable car. After this, old cobblestones lead you further into the deep valley of João-Gomes brook.

In a sharp right-hand bend in the cobbled path, a dirt path branches off to the left towards Levada dos Tornos, while signs further down the path point the way to Curral dos Romeiros and the Levada do Bom Sucesso. The route to Funchal described here follows the cobbled path down and round the bend to the right.

After this descent, a wide bridge **2** extends over the valley floor, before you start to climb again. About 5 minutes after the bridge, at an ascending left-hand hairpin bend in the cobbled road, fork off to the right

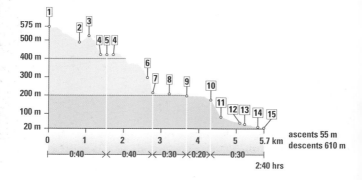

onto a narrow path **3** and into the forest; a sign on a lamppost ('Levada do Bom Sucesso') also shows the way.

After a short distance, a set of earth steps supported by wooden struts appears. At first, the steps alternate with level sections. Some 10 minutes after branching off from the cobbled path (at 3), the path reaches a strikingly round clearing which was presumably once the site of a coal pile. Your path continues on the other side. After a further set of earth steps another path crosses yours **4**. At this point, a short detour to a waterfall in an idyllic setting **5** is worth the effort: the entire excursion only takes 10 minutes.

Return via the same path to **4** and continue out of the valley. The route cuts across the slope on a more or less level course until earth steps lead downwards. The path cuts across the slope once again, and features further steep steps leading downwards as well as short ascents. Ignore a path to the left, as your route continues to head for the end of the valley.

At what appears to be a path branching off **6** to the left (marked with a heavily weathered 'X' composed of yellow and red stripes), continue down steps to the right. A brief, steep and rocky passage follows after a few steps, which then descend very sharply until they reach the levada **7**.

(At this point, you could take a **detour to the source of the levada** to the right, where an impressive valley basin and waterfall awaits in a side valley. However, in my research for the third edition of this book, the path was in such poor condition that I would advise against it.)

The path to Funchal follows the levada out through the valley, where it crosses a side valley with a narrow bridge (about 50 cm wide and 6 m long). Solid wire cable railings help with this ▶

Length/walking time: approx. 5.7 km, 2:40 hrs.

Terrain: the route is a steep descent on cobbled or dirt paths and steps, and can be very slippery in places. For some short sections along the Levada do Bom Sucesso, a head for heights is required – certain exposed sections are poorly secured. Surefootedness is a necessity for the entire route!

Marking: none, signs point the way in parts; yellow-red cross stripes were planned, but have only been sporadically implemented.

Equipment: sturdy walking shoes; poles make the long descent easier.

Supplies: take water. Stop for a bite at the start at the Café do Parque, Largo da Fonte or the Café do Monte by the summit station of the Monte – Funchal cable car 1, or by the ticket desk of the Monte – Jardim Botânico cable car. At the end of the route, Funchal features countless bars, cafés and restaurants, incl. the Restaurante Embaixador Madeirense as noted in the route description between 14 and 15.

Getting there: For drivers, I recommend leaving the car in Funchal and using public transport to get up to Monte due to its lack of parking spaces (car park by the valley station of the Funchal – Monte cable car), either with bus lines 20 or 21 (1 or 2x per hour) or the cable car, which runs continuously from 9.30am–6pm; bus line 22 runs once or twice per hour to its terminal, Babosas.

Walk 7

▶ crossing. Subsequent narrow sections of the levada wall are also secured by railings, but walkers should still take **particular caution** here. The levada then leads on along the rock face below overhanging rocks; the railings here are little more than decorative and offer no real protection. Below, in the valley, you can see the vast river engineering works carried out after the severe storm of 2010 to limit the destructive force of future torrents of water.

Where the levada leads between rock faces, use your **hands to balance yourself**. These rather tricky sections are concluded by another, shorter, solid concrete bridge with railings **8**.

The gradient of the levada's descent increases near to the motorway, though the path leaves the levada for a short period almost directly under a high motorway bridge **9**. An old cobbled path leads slightly below it, but meets the levada again a few steps later. Passing small field terraces, your route continues towards Funchal and, at a street around 20 minutes after the last bridge, the levada section ends and the descent into the city begins.

Don't follow the street to the left but instead go down the steps to the right which, though they may appear private, are in fact public. These

The rustic Levada do Bom Sucesso above the island's capital, Funchal

steps then become a narrow path lined with street lamps by the name of Bêco da Portada de Ferro. At the end of this path, a short set of steps leads down to the ER 102 **10**, the road between Funchal and the Jardim Botânico.

If you wish to end the walk here, follow this road upwards and, a few minutes later, you come to a bus stop served by regular buses to the Funchal coast road. However, if you wish to continue on foot, walk down the street for a few metres to the right where, on the left, there is a footpath with steps, the 2ª Travessa da Ribeira de João Gomes.

This concrete path leads past several picturesque, wild and romantic gardens. Ignore paths branching off from yours; if in doubt, continue straight on until the footpath reaches the arterial road **11** from Funchal towards the motorway, where you bear left towards the city.

The following section is less attractive, with lots of traffic! Walk past a petrol station; if possible, keep on the footpath on the left side of the street, though it is often full of parked cars.

Pass to the left of a street bridge leading into a tunnel, after which some steps **12** to the right lead down to a bus stop directly beneath the bridge. Continue past this and down towards the city. Your route passes by a pleasant square paved with pebbles **13** by the Centro Dr. Agostinho Cardoso; after the pedestrian crossing, you can amble through a small **park** with a bronze statue of a peasant woman in the middle. The end of the park also features a magnificent dragon tree (→ p. 15).

After the park, head left onto Rua Miguel Carvalho, which leads to a roundabout in front of the Liceu de Jaime Moniz. On the other side, continue down the Rua do Arcipreste.

At Largo das Torneiras **14**, you firstly pass Rua Latina Coelho before Rua dos Barreiros leads into Funchal's old town. Walk past Travessa de Amoreira until you come to Rua de Santa Maria; on the corner with Rua dos Barreiros is the Restaurante Embaixador Madeirense (✆ 291-224655; good local cuisine). Immediately after, the street comes to the valley station **15** of the cable car to Monte, which marks the end of the route. ■

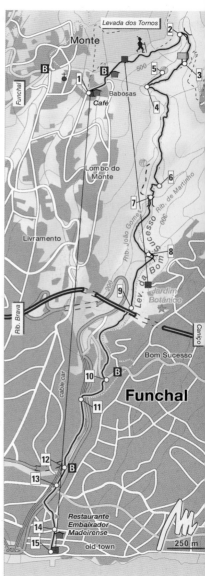

*** Along the adventure-packed Levada do Castelejo

Starting from the ER 101 (Porto da Cruz – Portela), this route runs along the Levada do Castelejo and into the Ribeiro Frio valley – a varied day-long walk between fields to an idyllic river valley.

▶▶ The starting point lies on the ER 108 from Porto da Cruz over the Portela Pass by the turnoff **1** to Cruz da Guarda.

The entrance to the levada is on this road: walk against the flow and head straight towards the distinctive Eagle Rock. The levada leads past a few isolated houses and small field terraces.

> **Variant 1: Gentle * Along the Levada do Castelejo to Cruz**
>
> If you don't have a head for heights, it's better to limit yourself to the first section from 1 to 8. If you're travelling by bus, it's best to walk down to Cruz 13, so that you don't have to walk the whole way back. And, of course, car drivers can avoid having to do so by taking a taxi from Cruz back to the start.

After a few minutes, the path leads through a short, low tunnel **2**. It is in good condition, and you don't need a torch. On the other side of the tunnel, the levada leads into an uninhabited valley. The levada represents a vital connecting route between individual districts for local residents, and is lined by street lights as a result.

Your route continues along the levada, ignoring paths and steps

Houses by the Levada do Castelejo

that branch off, as they only lead to houses or fields. Further into the unpopulated valley, a short bridge **3** leads over the valley floor. In a second arm of the valley, another bridge **4** again crosses the valley floor.

At this point, your route briefly departs from the levada but joins it again soon after. On leaving the valley to the north-west, a precipitous section often subject to landslides must be traversed, though railings make the path safe.

In the next valley, the levada passes by a few isolated houses, beyond which another concrete bridge leads over the valley floor.

Then, in the next large valley, a road runs through the far section. A short tunnel **5** first runs about 15 m under the road before a bend leads out of the valley and into another, uninhabited valley. Some of the terraces here lie idle, and only a few are actively farmed.

After this valley, a left-hand curve **6** provides a wonderful view of the striking **Eagle Rock (Penha de Águia)**. A few metres further on, the route leads past a water basin and **a very steep slope**. It is 20 m long, and stepping stones on the levada then make the following 15 m easier, and the path soon becomes wider and much easier to walk along.

After other small and rather unremarkable valleys, the levada runs past houses and crosses a narrow cul-de-sac **7**. (If you would like to end the route here, follow this route down for about 10 minutes to reach the ER 108 and enjoy refreshments at the Bar Adega da Cruz at 13.)

After crossing the narrow cul-de-sac, the valley land becomes increasingly heavily farmed. In summer, it is considerably greener than the previous valleys. The levada skirts the houses of the district of **Terra do Baptista**. Then cross another road **8** ▶

Length/walking time: approx. 14.4 km there and back to Cruz 13 in 4:20 hrs.; there and all the way back to 1 is about 17.8 km, 5:30 hrs.

Terrain: on the whole, a demanding long-distance route; only the initial levada section is easy. From the Ribeiro Frio 9 valley on, a head for heights and surefootedness are required; exposed sections are not protected in parts and the path is prone to landslides. Such damage is normally repaired quickly, but if in doubt or if landslides have occurred, avoid such sections. Do not attempt this route in rain or strong winds!

Marking: none, but the path is clear.

Equipment: sturdy walking shoes, poles provide balance in the Ribeiro Frio valley.

Supplies: take drinking water; option to take a break in Cruz at the Bar Adega da Cruz 13.

Getting there: by car, take the Machico – Santana motorway (Via Expresso), exit for Porto da Cruz/Portela. From there, drive up towards Portela. The walk begins in the district of Referta (no signs), directly by the turnoff to Cruz da Guarda (also signposted as 'Quinta da Capela'). Rising from below, the road makes a sharp right-hand bend at this point, and this is where the levada crosses. Bus → p. 27. Taxi rank in Machico ✆ 291-962480, in Faial ✆ 291-572416.

Walk 8

▶ where a metal sign ('Levada do Castelejo') shows the path continuing along the levada. A little later, the path reaches the last house, and the levada bends into the striking Ribeiro Frio valley **9**. In clear conditions, you can see the Pico do Arieiro and the Pico das Torres.

Caution: The following section to the source of the levada requires **surefootedness and a head for heights**. The tricky passages are protected by railings but still require care and attention.

A couple of minutes after the levada bends into the deep valley, the route reaches its first exposed area. Around 80 m long and made safe with railings, it is followed by another exposed passage, though the latter is shorter and is also secured. In a left-hand bend, a rock **10** protrudes onto the path at around shoulder height. Psychologically, this section might be tricky as, despite the railings, it's impossible to see what's up ahead.

Slowly but surely, you approach the riverbed down to the right, until you reach a large boulder **11** that obstructs the path along the levada. To bypass this obstacle, take the steps to the right down to the riverbed before a short, stony path leads to the start of the levada **12**.

The large rocks in the riverbed, which have been eroded and rounded over time, are a perfect spot for a rest. In summer, though, almost all of the water is directed into the levada. If you would like to walk further, follow the signs

---

Variant 2: Adventurous ✱✱✱
From Cruz along the Levada do Castelejo to its source

If you're looking for a challenge, focus on the section in the Ribeiro Frio valley (take the ER 101 to Cruz and park by the Bar Adega da Cruz → Walk 9/Getting there, p. 69). Signs point towards a narrow cul-de-sac that continues to ascend straight on until crossed by the levada (after about 15 minutes); then follow the description from ⑦.

from here to Lombo Grande toward São Roque do Faial on the other side of the valley. (From the left of the levada spring, follow a rocky forest trail upwards that leads above the water supply – and where you can at least cool off your feet. In some places, the rockpools are so deep that you can sit in the water.)

The same route then leads back to the start. After about 1 hour, the path reaches the first houses and, 5 minutes later, crosses the road **8** and continues along the levada to a steep cul-de-sac **7**. (If you are not walking back to the starting point, bear left here.) ▶

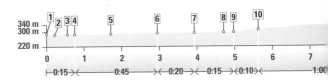

▶ The narrow tarmac road descends steeply over a ridge. At a road junction from the left, continue straight on for a short while until you reach the ER 101 **13** in the district of **Cruz**. On the right is the bus stop with the Bar Adega da Cruz opposite. ■

Stunning views of Eagle Rock on the gentle variant

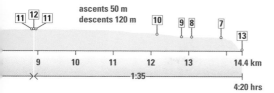

The marker stone on Eagle Roc

This short yet demanding rocky mountain hike leads from Cruz over the most prominent mass of rock on the north coast and down to Penha de Águia de Baixo.

✶✶✶✶ Scaling
Eagle Rock

▶▶ The starting point is on regional road ER 108 between Porto da Cruz and Faial. Beyond the Bar Adega da Cruz, at almost the road's highest point in the district of **Cruz**, a signpost **1** points in the direction of Eagle Rock ('Vereda da Penha de Águia').

Walk a short distance along the narrow Caminho da Cruz village road until you come to a fork.

Here, walk a few metres to the right, then take a left at a house and climb three steps to reach a narrow village levada (directly behind the Bar Adega da Cruz). Your route follows the levada towards Eagle Rock until earth and rock steps **2** branch off to the left and a sign points towards Penha de Águia.

After a few steps, the path reaches a ridge which you climb to the right. In a mixed forest featuring acacias, pines and eucalyptus trees, the path briefly levels out, though overall it continues to climb.

Keep right at a fork **3** as the path to the left only leads down to some fields. A few steps later, bear right again at another fork – steep, rocky sections lie in wait not far ahead. On your climb, you will have to negotiate tree heath and heather, bend after bend and rock step after rock step. Near the summit, the path comes to a steep channel, and there are more rocky steps to climb before reaching a saddle **4** on Eagle Rock. ▶

Length/walking time: approx. 2.9 km, 2:25 hrs.

Terrain: one-way hike with very steep incline, steep rock steps in elevated sections. Descent slippery in places on rocky dirt path. So long as you don't venture to the edge at the summit marker (something we explicitly discourage!), the route features no vertiginous passages. **However, surefootedness is crucial!**

Marking: none.

Equipment: sturdy walking shoes, sun and rain protection, poles.

Supplies: take water. Bar Adega da Cruz at the start ⑤ with outdoor seating; Bar-Restaurante Galé ⑧ with outdoor seating, open daily, ✆ 291-572501, at the end of the route in Penha de Águia de Baixo.

Getting there: by car, take the Via Expresso between Machico and Porto da Cruz, exit for 'Porto da Cruz Oeste'. Then head for Terra Baptista and Campo de Futebol. Just before the road's highest point is the Bar Adega da Cruz, where a sign points towards the Eagle Rock ('Vereda da Penha de Água'). Bus → p. 27.

Getting back: from Penha de Águia de Baixo, take the taxi back (€6, taxi rank in Machico ✆ 291-962480, in Faial ✆ 291-572416). Alternatively, walk to regional road ER 101 and take the bus from there (→ p. 27). The road back to ① is 3 km, takes 45 mins and is virtually traffic-free. After almost 2 km, the road to Porto da Cruz passes through a tunnel. Before this, bear right on the 'old' road (sign: 'Terra Baptista') which soon leads back to ①.

The view of Madeira's mountainous landscape from the summit

▶ At the saddle, keep left and head north-east; cross a slope covered by eucalyptus forest before the final climb which – though gentler – again leads through tree heath bushes. The route then leads directly to the summit marker **5** of **Eagle Rock**, where there are magnificent views of the villages along the north coast and, in good visibility, of the island's highest peaks. Even those with a good head for heights should stay clear of the edge: the southern face of the Eagle Rock features a vertical drop, the vegetation's appearance belies the protection it offers and the rock on Madeira is brittle (→ p. 11).

From here, you go down the less steep western face of Eagle Rock. From the summit marker, your route essentially follows the continuation of the path you climbed, as earth steps supported by wooden beams lead downwards.

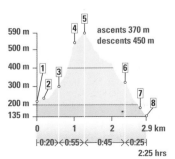

After about 5 minutes, there is a clear view of Faial and the path becomes somewhat steeper, though fallen trees may lie across it. The path then becomes almost pleasantly flat on a hillside covered in ferns, but watch out for holes near the edge!

Further down, the path leads out of the forest before bending to the left and running across the slopes above the sea through tree heath and heather bushes.

At a clearing **6**, a left-hand bend provides a lovely view over the roaring Atlantic and the small village of Sítio Penha de Águia de Baixo, this route's destination.

However, some steep turns still remain, before a concrete stairway lined with street lights begins at a first small house **7**, and you follow it to continue your descent. Cross a concrete road and continue downwards.

The footpath ends at the thoroughfare in the village of **Sítio da Penha de Águia de Baixo** directly by Restaurant Galé **8**. You can take this opportunity for a snack or to call a taxi; otherwise, walk along the village road for about 20 minutes to regional road ER 101 (in this section, VE 1), which is served by buses. ■

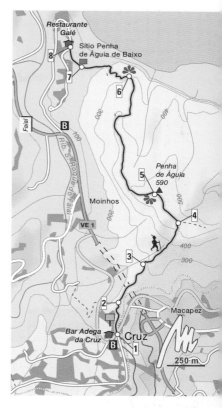

✳✳✳ Variant: up and down Eagle Rock

If you only plan to climb Eagle Rock and descend via the same route, do so from Sítio da Penha de Águia de Baixo, the end of the route described here – the route used to climb the summit in this route is decidedly difficult to descend. To do so, start in the village of Penha de Águia de Baixo (by car, cross the bridge below Faial on the ER 101 or come off the VE 1). Street parking is available near Restaurant Galé, and the route then starts just to the right of the restaurant 8. Climb some steps to reach a concrete footpath lined by street lights that ends at the last house. Here, keep left and continue to climb, and follow the directions in reverse order. The route is clear and should be easy to find by following the description in reverse order (ascent about 1:30 hrs, descent approx 1 hr).

*** From Ribeiro Frio to the Portela pass

Classic, wild and romantic walk from Ribeiro Frio along the 200-year-old Levada do Furado through natural laurel forest. At the end, the route passes the Lamaceiros lodge with its beautiful gardens.

▶▶ The starting point is regional road ER 103 in **Ribeiro Frio**. Beside the Restaurante Ribeiro Frio, a metal sign **1** points the way to Portela.

> **Tip**
>
> Between 10.30am and midday, Ribeiro Frio becomes congested due to island tour buses stopping. If you want to walk in peace or stop for a quiet bite, arrive before or after this time.

A few steps down the paved footpath is a wooden sign, after which there is a bridge over a stream that is also called Ribeiro Frio. An information board provides an overview of the route; the estimated walking time of 5 hours given here is very generous.

Wide, extended concrete steps lead down to the levada path, as you enter the humid world of the laurel forest (→ p. 16). Walkers should hope for sunny, dry weather, as this makes the walk considerably easier – though such conditions are not the norm. To begin with, the path is wide and poses no difficulties.

However, the route's first narrow passages soon follow, and it passes a draining tunnel **2** sealed by an iron gate.

A period of alternating narrow passes and broader section of path then follows, with the exposed areas made safe. It is then worth pausing for a break at a bridge **3** leading over a tributary, as suitable locations are rare in the subsequent narrow section of the route.

After crossing the bridge, a large rock lies on the path. A few steps behind this, keep your balance along the levada wall around a

The tunnel at waypoint ⑨

bend with solid wire cable railings. You can also hold onto the rock to the right. Continue through the following narrow but straight passages.

Then, **take care**: the first narrow, crumbly curve in the levada must be bypassed. A set of steps **4** protected with wire cable railings leads into the valley floor to the left, where a small pool has developed. This bypass is only a few steps long, but can be devilishly **slippery**.

On the other side, carefully laid steps lead back up to the levada. A few minutes later, a second detour follows through the valley floor, but this section is also very brief. There are other narrow passages further along the levada, but they are all well protected, and often lead directly along the levada wall.

A little later, the levada flows through a few crevices in the rock where concrete stepping stones make it easier to get through.

After a **shrine to the Virgin Mary 5**, watch out again: a path leads down to the valley floor and rejoins the levada on the other side. However, as this section of the levada has been repaired, you can continue along the wall and thereby walk around a narrow valley. (If the railings are missing, then it is perhaps better to opt for the detour.)

Afterwards, the path becomes wide once again, which is certainly a welcome break, though further narrow passages await up ahead. At the point where rocks **6** block the path directly along the levada, a clear trail leads below the levada. The start of the next detour from the levada at another narrow spot is clearly identifiable. A set of carefully laid steps leads back ▶

Length/walking time: approx. 10.4 km, 3:20 hrs.

Terrain: the path is in good condition. Exposed and narrow sections are well protected, but **surefootedness is required** as long stretches lead over rocky ground. You might feel dizzy at certain places, but these areas are actually well protected.

Marking: none, but the route is clear. Official designation: 'PR 10, Levada do Furado'. There are signs in some places on the descent to Portela.

Equipment: sturdy walking shoes, rain protection, warm clothing; torch, though tunnels can be negotiated without one.

Supplies: take water. Stop for a bite at the start at Restaurante Ribeiro Frio (formerly Victor's Bar), ☎ 291-575898, trout specials, daily 9am–7pm. At the end by the Portela pass **17**: Restaurante Miradouro da Portela, ☎ 291-966169, meat skewer specials; Restaurante Portela à Vista with outdoor seating and lovely panorama dining room, ☎ 291-963189, also has meat skewer specials, a popular weekend dining destination. Both usually open daily until about 6pm.

Getting there: by car, from the south, head over the Poiso pass to Ribeiro Frio and park by the trout farm. Taxis (approx. €30) in Santana ☎ 291-572540. Bus → p. 27.

Getting back: Taxis generally stop at the Portela pass or can be called from one of the nearby restaurants. Journey (30 mins) from Portela pass to Ribeiro Frio approx. €30; taxi rank in Machico ☎ 291-962480, in Faial ☎ 291-572416. Bus → p. 27.

Walk 10

▶ also up to the water channel **7**, after which the route again descends into a valley floor as another bend in the levada is impassable.

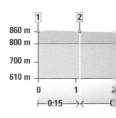

A little later, the levada bends sharply to the right **8**. To the left, a path branches off towards a rocky outcrop from where, in good visibility (which is rare), walkers can enjoy views of the island's highest peaks. If you feel the need, this is a good spot for a second break.

Some distance further on, the levada flows into a vast crevice **9**, which is actually a high tunnel. You briefly follow the channel, which is equipped with stepping stones, through the mountain. A torch can be helpful here, but isn't absolutely essential.

A **spectacular passage** then follows, as the levada leads into the vertical rock face. Railings make the path secure, and though several short tunnels through the rock face must be traversed, a torch is still not necessary.

After passing this rock face, the path widens and leads you to the rustic water house **10** of Lamaceiros, which is reminiscent of a prison tower. To its left is a new levada cleaning station. Follow the levada a little further, and you reach a crossing – which is also part of Walk 4 (→ p. 46). At this crossing, follow the signs towards Portela down to the left where, a few steps further, a narrow levada joins your path.

At an inconspicuous fork in the path **11**, keep left and climb a narrow set of steps directly beside the narrow levada to the beautiful gardens in front of the **lodge** **12**, the Posto Forestal of Lamaceiros, and a handful of picnic tables. Your route continues on the wide forest path, past the lodge and descending gently above a reservoir.

We pass the access road to the reservoir and reach a lovely viewpoint **13** with views of the prominent **Eagle Rock (Penha de Águia)** to the north-east. Then continue down a wide, unsurfaced road up to a fork **14** in a long, gradual right-hand bend near a large, enclosed area farmed by Herdade Lombo

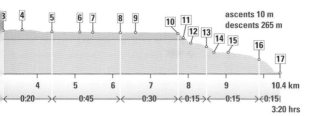

das Faias. At this fork, your route leaves the wide road and bears left (following signs for 'Portela') on a path that leads past the enclosed area.

A short, gentle uphill section then follows. In a right-hand bend **15**, the concrete levada again runs alongside the path which can be very slippery in wet weather. Follow this path to a set of earth steps **16**. (At this point, you can see the remains of a former levada house and a narrow branch of the levada leads away to the right.) The short set of steps leads down to the left, and the subsequent dirt path is then permeated by tree roots and rocks. It ends at the road from the Portela pass to Santo da Serra.

Follow this street downhill a short distance to reach the Portela pass **17**. ■

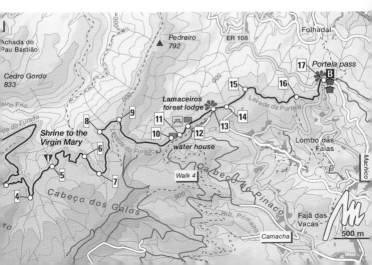

* To the Balcões viewpoint

An easy walk through the laurel forest along the old Levada da Serra do Faial to a truly spectacular viewpoint.

▶▶ The starting point is in **Ribeiro Frio**, below the Restaurant Ribeiro Frio, where the levada meets regional road ER 103. At the start of the levada, a board **1** provides information on the route and signs point the way.

Walk along a wide path that runs beside the levada to the north, against the water flow and through the laurel forest.

A little later, the channel flows through a vast opening **2** and, soon after, passes the Bar Flor da Selva **3**.

A little further on, you pass the Balcões Bar; now closed, it has certainly seen better days.

A concrete footpath **4** branches off to the right at a natural stone cottage, but your path continues to follow the levada as it flows through another large opening. A wooden sign then points the way to the Balcões viewpoint.

Magnificent view from Balcões

Fish farming in Ribeiro Frio

A little later, the levada bends to the left **5** where the path beside it is blocked off. A cobbled path, signposted with 'Balcões', branches off to the right and falls gently to reach the spectacular **viewpoint** at **Balcões 6**.

The views extend to the island's highest peaks: on the left are the red-white masts of Pico do Arieiro; to the right of this, in a saddle, is the prominent peak of the Pico do Gato. Further to the right is the rugged Pico das Torres, and even further right is the less imposing Pico Ruivo (where even the mountain shelter can be spotted). In the valley far below is the Fajã da Nogueira hydroelectric power station.

The route then returns to the start via the same route. ■

Length/walking time: total of 2.6 km, out and back 1 hr.
Terrain: easy levada walk on a wide path. In wet conditions, route may be slippery.
Marking: none. The path's official designation is PR 11.
Equipment: sturdy walking shoes.
Supplies: take water; Bar Flor da Selva 3 has a souvenir shop and a lovely little terrace but limited seating.
Getting there: by taxi or car, take regional road ER 103 to Ribeiro Frio. Parking available opposite the Posto Florestal Ribeiro Frio lodge by the trout farm or by Restaurant Ribeiro Frio next to the bus stop. The bus (→ Timetable p. 23) is not recommendable for this tour due to the long journey times. Taxi rank in Santana ✆ 291-572540; Santana – Ribeiro Frio approx. €25.
Tip: Ribeiro Frio is a popular destination. From about 10.30am onwards, numerous tourists buses stop here, but beforehand or late afternoon you'll basically have Riberio Frio to yourself.

Walk 11

ascents 10 m
(one-way)

1 2 3 4 5 6
855 m
845 m

0   1 1.3 km
├─0:15─>├<0:15─┤
            0:30 hrs

*** Circular coastal walk from Santana

Strenuous ups and down on old cobbled paths. Highlights include an adventurous detour to a former jetty, the Calhau de São Jorge, as well as an open-air pool.

►► The starting point is the restaurant at Quinta do Furão on the north-west outskirts of **Santana**. Those travelling by bus should alight at the signposted turnoff to Quinta **1** (let the bus driver know in advance). From the fork, the hotel car park is about 300 m away. At the large car park, signs point the way to the hotel restaurant. Directly in front of the restaurant entrance, a path to the left leads past a panoramic terrace and up to a wooden railing.

This is where the old **coastal path** begins. At first, it runs along the coastal cliff landscape, past several vineyards to the Hotel Quinta do Furão. Your route practically circles the hotel, following the wooden fence at all times until it ends at a fenced piece of land **2**.

Continue straight on along the coast and down a narrow dirt path, always staying to the right of the fence. The path is not protected in this section, but the steep break-off edge is overgrown.

At the point where the path starts to lead downhill, look out for steps

Vineyard by the Hotel Quinta do Furão

to the left leading down to a road, which you then follow for a short time. The old cobbled path **3** leading to Calhau de São Jorge forks off sharply to the right. A temporary signpost points towards São Jorge and Calhau. The cobbled path first passes houses before a levada crosses the path a few minutes later **4**.

The path then descends more steeply over round cobblestones. In a series of bends, the old – yet skilfully designed – path winds its way to the valley floor of the Ribeira de São Jorge river. The cobbled path crosses the river over an old stone bridge **5** above the open-air pool before the path from the car park joins from the left. Follow the old cobbled path to the right where a set of steps soon leads down to a sunbathing area by the mouth of the river and a shingle beach.

As the path continues, it leads past derelict and renovated houses. At a spring **6** and some ruins, the path from São Jorge (the route by which you will later descend) joins from the left.

However, you carry straight on for the time being, as a sign points towards 'cais antigo'. ▶

Length/walking time: total (with shorter return route) approx. 9.8 km, 3:20 hrs; only up to São Jorge 5.3 km, 2:45 hrs.

Terrain: circular route on old cobbled paths, slippery when wet, long sections without shade. Cool, dry conditions are ideal for this route.

Variants: Another option for a circular route would be to start/finish at the car park at Calhau de São Jorge above the open-air pool 5.

Marking: none.

Equipment: sturdy walking shoes, sun and rain protection; in summer, consider swimwear for the open-air pool at Calhau de São Jorge.

Supplies: take water. Restaurant at Hotels Quinta do Furão (after 1), daily 12pm–3.30pm/7pm–9.30pm, www.quintadofurao.com, ✆ 291-570100. In summer, there is a bar by the swimming pool at Calhau de São Jorge near 5; in São Jorge, snack bar/restaurant Casa de Palha (→ Map), ✆ 291-576382, good local cuisine (incl. soups served in hollowed-out bread bowls). At the picnic area by 9 is the Café/Bar Cabo Aéreo, ✆ 291-575209.

Getting there: take the taxi or car to Santana. From there, continue on the ER 101 to the north-west outskirts of the town and the car park of the restaurant of Quinta do Furão (signposted as 'Achada do Gramacho' and 'Hotel Quinta do Furão'). Taxi rank in Santana ✆ 291-572540. Bus → p. 27/28.

Walk 12

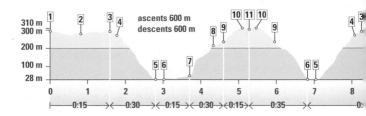

▶ Below a steep rock face, the path narrows as chunks of the path occasionally break off here, although it is relatively safe. A rather risky-looking wooden bridge crosses a steep side valley, which sometimes features a waterfall, before the path begins to climb.

Next is another section along the vertical rock face, but this time somewhat higher above the sea. The path here is relatively wide. Before reaching the old wharves, another old cobbled path **7** forks off and up towards São Jorge.

(If you're sure-footed with a head for heights, feel free to make the **descent to the jetty** – but the path does become narrow and also slippery after a left-hand bend. You can reach the headland via a concrete ramp, which doesn't look entirely safe, though locals often fish there – clearly they trust the ramp more than this author.)

Bathing at Calhau de São Jorge

The climb to São Jorge starts off relatively steeply, and after about 10 minutes reaches a short flat section where you can get your breath back. It then continues to a village road **8**, already part of São Jorge. Keep right, as the road descends at first, leading past field terraces. Then, rising gently, the road comes to a large paved picnic area **9** by the Café Cabo Aéreo. (If you don't wish to visit São Jorge, you can start the descent here.)

Two streets lead up from the picnic area: take the steeper one to the left, which immediately makes a sharp left-hand bend and, after a few more bends, passes the entrance to a **graveyard**. The narrow village street then continues to climb. After a few minutes, it passes a house with a thatched roof that has

9.8 km

3:20 hrs

been beautifully renovated. At a fork in the road **10**, continue straight on (Rua Dr. Leonel Mendoza, 'Medico Municipal'). Continue past another junction and, a few steps later, you reach the **church 11 of São Jorge**.

A little further, the road reaches the bus stop for line 103. (Here, the branch to the right leads to the car park of the **Restaurante Casa de Palha**. From the junction, follow the street up to the right, where the restaurant is situated in several thatched buildings.)

Straight ahead is regional road ER 101, where there are also bus stops for the return journey and some simple bars where you can stop for a bite. If you would prefer to walk – or if you have to – turn back down the path you climbed to the picnic area **9**, where the cobbled path down to Calhau de São Jorge starts.

The path is very well maintained; chunks have only broken away in the lower section, and the remaining path is certainly wide enough. After a series of bends, you reach the ruins and the spring **6** once again. The rest of the return journey to **Santana** along the route you walked earlier can be made in 1 hour, or the car park up from the swimming pool **5** can be reached in 5 minutes. ∎

*** From Queimadas to the Caldeirão Verde

This route leads through the laurel forest and follows an old levada the whole way. Though the outbound and return routes are identical, the different perspectives make both directions very interesting. The destination is the Caldeirão Verde, a green valley basin with a high waterfall.

▶▶ The starting point is at the houses in **Queimadas**. At the entrance to the forecourt **1** of two thatched houses, wooden signs ('Caldeirão Verde'/'Caldeirão do Inferno') point straight across the yard. At the other side, a wooden bridge leads over a duck pond to the levada, which runs beyond the pond. Here, signs show the way to Vale de Lapa and the Caldeirão Verde ('PR 9, 6.5 km').

To begin with, the path is wide and leads through a shady forest. A few minutes later, another track **2** – the Caminho dos Folhadeiros – crosses your route. A sign shows the way to Caldeirão Verde along the levada. The further you walk, the more typical the laurel forest (→ p. 16) scenery becomes: dark green shades dominate, the trees are strewn with beard lichen and the path is lined by large bushes of the endemic Madeira blueberry (→ p. 18).

Even if the slope to the right features dense greenery, you should continue to tread **with caution** as some sections feature vertical drops.

Bridge at waypoint 5

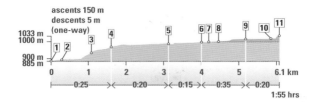

ascents 150 m
descents 5 m
(one-way)

However, particularly exposed sections are well protected.

After about 15 minutes, you have to leave the levada for a short time as it would be too dangerous to continue along the brittle, slippery wall. Clearly visible steps **3** lead down to the right at this point; follow them down and then continue along to a dirt path. As the path leads across a small ravine, glance up at the brittle levada wall above. A further set of concrete steps then leads back up to the levada.

After this detour, the path soon narrows and runs directly along the levada wall. Strong railings ensure that this section and the bridge **4** that follows, where the levada itself leads over a small gully, can be crossed safely. ▷

Length/walking time: identical outbound and return routes, approx. 12.2 km, 3:50 hrs; the 5:30 hrs shown on the board at **1** is inaccurate.

Terrain: head for heights required in some places! There are railings, but the path is narrow and the plunging views could make less experienced levada walkers feel queasy. Watch out for slippery roots in wet conditions.

Marking: none, but the path clearly runs along the levada at all times. Its official name is PR 9.

Equipment: it is important to remember a torch for the tunnel. Take rain protection even in good weather, as water drips from rock faces even in summer in the fog belt. Sturdy walking shoes are a necessity.

Supplies: no snack points, so take provisions and water; avoid drinking water from the levada.

Getting there: Queimadas is signposted from Santana. The higher you climb, the steeper and narrower the road becomes. In the humid laurel forest region, it is covered in moss in parts — skid hazard! At the weekend, it is best to park further down on the wider parts of the road, or drive up to the house above the park itself. Its yard is sometimes open and, if so, parking should be permitted. No buses; taxis in Santana, ☎ 291-572540.

Walk 13

Through the humid tunnel

► Soon after, the route becomes wider and easier to walk on, though thick tree heath stems grow horizontally across the path in places.

The path then narrows once again, and leads into a valley with a **picturesque waterfall** and a bridge **5** leading over the valley floor.

A bit later, you come to the first tunnel **6**. It is curved and low, which means that the exit isn't immediately visible – yet the other side is quickly reached.

Shortly after, a path forks off to the right (signposted with 'Achada do Tuco' and 'Ilha, 3.8 km'), but your route to the Caldeirão Verde continues along the levada and into a tunnel **7**. This one is somewhat longer, but the exit can be seen straight away. The lower sections are rather tricky, but they are quickly negotiated and the next tunnel follows immediately.

This tunnel **8** is the most challeging on the route: yet although it is longer, lower and more winding than the others, it

also features 'peep holes' with lovely views into the steep, green valley. It only takes a few minutes to get through it.

After the tunnel, the path runs about 2 m below the levada and is well protected beside the vertical wall. It then comes to the last, very short tunnel **9**.

As the path approaches its destination the green scenery to either side becomes increasingly impressive. Just before the Caldeirão Verde, a steep, narrow side valley must be negotiated.

The branch off to the Caldeirão Verde is marked by a river valley with a wide water slide **10** paved with rough stones that only carries water after heavy rainfall. A narrow path leads above the valley to the **Caldeirão Verde 11** in about 2 minutes. The area directly by the waterfall and the large stones beside it, most of which are dry, are ideal spots to take a break. The return route then follows the same path in reverse. ■

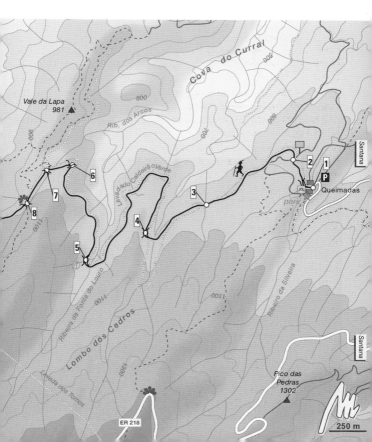

** Along the Levada do Rei into the Ribeiro Bonito valley

The levada's route, which is sometimes very challenging in places, runs along the vertical rock face for long sections. However, it is fairly well protected which makes it possible for walkers to experience an otherwise inaccessible picturesque valley relatively easily.

►► The **approach road from São Jorge** ends by widening into a large clearing, from which the trail begins to the left. An information board **1** provides details of the route along the levada. (The stated altitude of 710 metres at the end of the levada is, however, inaccurate.) The sign 'Levada do Rei, PR 18' shows the way along the track, which is lined by streetlights. The levada flows to the right of the path from the start.

View tip

The detour via the lodge (from **4** on the return journey) is only worthwhile in fine conditions with good visibility, as the route then provides lovely views of the natural, green mountains on Madeira's northern slope.

After only a short time, turn right onto a lane **2** and walk to an oblong-shaped water basin, where a sign ('Ribeiro Bonito, 5.1 km') points the way. Before reaching the water basin, the lane bends to the right, but you should walk along the long side of the basin. On the other side of the water basin, a narrow

At waypoint **7**, water falls onto the levada wall

meadow path leads to steep steps heading up and along the levada.

At the end of the steps, the levada runs almost on a level. Your path follows it to the left into the valley, against the water flow.

After about 15 minutes, you cross a path **3** but continue along the levada. There are several exposed sections with a vertical drop to the left, though these are well protected with wire cable railings.

In a valley floor, where the levada bends sharply to the left, a wide, rocky path partly overgrown with grass comes down from the right to join yours **4**. At this point, you leave the levada on the return route in order to climb to the Posto Florestal São Jorge lodge and take in the beautiful views.

For now, however, you continue along the levada (signposted as 'Ribeiro Bonito, PR 18, 2.4 km'), where the path is almost as wide as a road.

A little later, another wide forest track meets yours in a side valley **5**, after which the path along the levada narrows once again. Soon after, the path reaches a small tunnel **6** which, though curved, is so short (barely 15 m) that you can see the light at the ▶

Length/walking time: approx. 9.6 km, 3:20 hrs.

Terrain: there are some exposed elevated sections along the Levada do Rei, though most are made safe with wire cable railings; in some less secure sections, the sheer wall is overgrown with plants. However, a **head for heights is beneficial**. Tread carefully. The climb to the lodge and subsequent descent are on wide forest tracks.

Marking: none; occasional signs. The path along the Levada do Rei is officially called PR 18; the unmarked return route via the lodge is not an official footpath.

Equipment: sturdy walking shoes. Rain protection is advisable even on sunny days due to the waterfall.

Supplies: no snack points along the route; take water and provisions.

Getting there: by car, take the ER 101 from São Jorge towards Cabanas/Arco de São Jorge. After São Jorge (about 2.5 km from the signposted exit to the church in São Jorge), just beyond the highest point on the road and near a bus shelter, a street branches off to the left (signs for 'Watermill' and 'Levada'). After about 600 m on this side road is a fork — bear right! After another 600 m, good parking facilities exist at the end of the road.

Caution: Heading from São Jorge, if you miss the (signposted) turning for Casa das Proteas and find yourself in a dead-straight alley of thuja trees, you've gone too far. Bus → p. 28.

Walk 14

▶ other end right from the start – but mind your head!

Immediately after the tunnel, there follows an exposed, narrow section of path made safe by railings, concrete slabs have also been laid on the levada to broaden the path. Beyond that is a **section without railings**. Though the edge with a vertical drop may feature extensive vegetation, you should still tread carefully in this section! The following exposed passages are then better secured. Despite the railings, a head for heights is a necessity in some places.

Somewhat further on, a **waterfall 7** rains down onto the levada wall. Stepping stones mean you can weave your way about 10 m behind the waterfall. The path is very slippery in this section; the water flow may be greater or lesser depending on the season, and even in summer you should expect a shower.

A little later, your path reaches the **Ribeiro Bonito** river **8**, which flows through a narrow, steep valley and is channelled almost entirely into the levada. You can pause for a break on the large stones at this wild and romantic location.

Then follow the same path back for a good portion of the route, until you reach the rocky path **4** leading up to the left. In good visibility, opt for the return path via the Posto Florestal São Jorge lodge. To do so, leave the levada at this point and follow the wide track upwards.

After about 2 minutes' climb, a stream **9** crosses the wide track; it may prove difficult to cross if the area has seen heavy rainfall. There are no further obstacles beyond this point.

After a tough yet brief incline, the path comes to a wide dirt track **10**. Take a right turn, and continue on an almost flat path. Two minutes later, another track joins from the left. Don't turn off here: continue straight on, where the track climbs and two further tracks join in quick succession (but again, do not turn off).

Continue straight on along a fairly level track which later begins to rise gently.

After a short, flat section, the wide access road **11** to the São Jorge lodge joins from the right: walk 100 m along it to the lodge's garden. In the garden is a prominent summit marker **12** painted black and white, from which there are extensive views of the dark green mountainsides.

Rock-face levada safety

Steep sections of the Levada do Rei make it one of Madeira's most spectacular levadas; new wire cable railings have now made it accessible for casual walkers.

From the lodge, return to the track and continue straight downhill, ignoring other tracks crossing yours and paths branching off to the side. The main track leads directly back to the starting point **1**. ∎

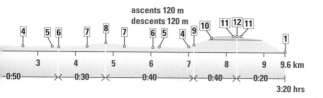

ascents 120 m
descents 120 m

| 4 | 5 6 | 7 | 8 | 7 | 6 5 | 4 9 | 10 | 11 12 11 | 1 |

3   4   5   6   7   8   9   9.6 km

0:50 ─── ✕ ─── 0:30 ─── ✕ ─── 0:40 ─── ✕ ─── 0:40 ─── ✕ ─── 0:20 ───

3:20 hrs

In the late 19th century, the King of Portugal ordered the construction of numerous cobbled paths on Madeira, including this coastal route, which led around the entire island. This route runs along a particularly well maintained section of the path.

✳✳ Along the north coast path from Arco de São Jorge to Boaventura

▶▶ The starting point is by the western exit from **Arco de São Jorge** by Restaurante Arco **1**. The path is signposted 'Caminho da Entrosa' from regional road ER 101: walk past the bar and restaurant, following signs, and you soon come to the old King's Path along the coast. The path undulates gently across the steep slopes as it follows the coastline. Initially, it passes by several wine terraces and fruit gardens, only some of which are actively farmed.

Leaving the fields behind, the further you progress, the more prevalent the natural coastal vegetation becomes, e.g. globularia, aeoniums and smooth spear-leaved spurge (→ p. 15).

We then climb gently beneath a steep rock face, where the path is wide and protected by solid metal railings. Shortly after the highest point **2**, there are lovely views into the valley of the Ribeira do Porco river, of the Restaurant São Cristóvão and even as far as Porto Moniz in the north-west of the island.

Our descent then begins along a winding road. This route demonstrates the craft of the old road builders, as the King's Path hugs the vertical wall through tight bends. After this rock face, it continues to wind into the valley of Ribeira do Porco. Before reaching the valley floor, concrete steps **3** branch off to a road to the left. ▶

Length/walking time: return route approx. 3.6 km, 2:00 hrs.

Terrain: easy route on an old cobbled path. Precipitous passages are made safe with railings. In wet conditions, these cobbles are very slippery. Risk of falling rocks in some places. Ask at Bar Arco whether the path is walkable. It's not unusual for parts of the path to break away.

Marking: none.

Equipment: sturdy walking shoes, sun and rain protection – the north coast is generally rather damp.

Supplies: take water. At the start of the walk: Bar-Restaurante Arco, Sítio da Enseada, ☏ 291-578149; at the turning point [6]: Restaurante São Cristóvão, ☏ 291-863031, well-kept restaurant with good, local cuisine (main courses €8–12) and snacks in the bar.

Getting there: though various bus routes pass by, the times are not convenient for walkers (→ Timetable p. 28). This route is much better suited to walkers with rental cars. By car, take the ER 101 to Arco de São Jorge; from there, head to the west of the village and Restaurant Arco.

Note: landslides are a common event in the vicinity of the steep rock face.

Walk 15

The views span scenic peaks and valleys and stretch to Boaventura

▶ To the right, a **detour** to a wide outcrop over the sea and the ruins of an old sugar cane factory is certainly worth the trip. For this diversion, leave the King's Path via the steps leading to a dirt track. Flat at first as it leads along a natural stone wall, the track soon comes to a wide rocky spur directly above the roaring surf.

At the end of this outcrop, steps branch off to the left and lead to a path that runs between the remains of the old **sugar cane factory**. Though the buildings are in a state of serious disrepair, their stately

past is still recognisable. Beyond the ruins, the path narrows as it moves towards the sea. However, if earth has slipped away, turn around! Some very slippery steps **4** cut into the tuff rock provide access to the coarse shingle beach, though it is too dangerous to bathe here.

Then, follow the same route back to the old King's Path and follow it down to the right, past some more ruins and over a picturesque **natural stone bridge**. (Directly by the start of the bridge, a narrow path forks off to the right and leads down into the river valley below, but looks too unsafe and narrow to me; I would advise against it.)

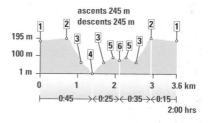

Beyond the bridge, climb up to a narrow path **5** branching off to the right, where the King's Path starts again. A sign for a 'Bar/Restaurant' hidden in a bush points the way to your next milestone.

After about 5 m, your path reaches a barely used levada. The path soon leaves this levada and leads down to the right, becoming more of a narrow beaten track through a meadow where conditions can be muddy and slippery. However, it soon comes to the car park of the Restaurant São Cristóvão **6**, where you follow the same path back to the starting point. ■

Skilful construction: the King's Paths on Madeira

In the late 19th century, the King of Portugal had numerous cobbled paths built on Madeira in the hope that improved infrastructure would encourage trade and agriculture. One of these new routes was a coastal path that led around the entire island. As the coast is generally composed of vertical drops into the ocean, many walls had to be built in the rock faces, to create a vaguely level surface. Small ledges were sometimes used as a foundation for the wall. The space between the wall and cliffs was then filled with rubble and debris, and the resulting path was later paved with basalt stones. The paths along the sheer coast are often little more than wide natural stone walls. The coastal path not only served as a connecting route, but was also intended to function as a lookout in order to be able to defend against attacks from sea more effectively and quickly. Unfortunately, most parts of the path later fell victim to road building works, or simply fell away into the sea. However, this section along the north coast is in good condition and has been repaired many times in the past.

*** Over the Pico Ruivo and down the northern face to Ilha

Such rich, varied walks are few and far between: an easy climb up the Pico Ruivo, Madeira's highest summit at 1,862 m, magnificent views in every direction and a long descent through an array of vegetation zones in the north of the island down to Ilha.

▶▶ The starting point is the large, unsurfaced car park **1** by the **Achada do Teixeira**. A board at the entrance to the footpath provides information on the section of the route up the Pico Ruivo and back down. From the car park, the signposted path ('PR 1.2, Pico Ruivo, 2.8 km') recently paved with natural stones begins to climb to the west. After about 5 minutes, a short flat section to the left provides views into the valley of Fajã da Nogueira and over to the Pico do Arieiro (→ Walk 17).

Another flat section follows and gives a glimpse of the jagged Pico das Torres. To the right of the path is the first mountain shelter, after which the path descends. To the left of a second shelter is a small spring **2** with drinkable water.

A few steps' climb leads to another flat section with a view of the mountain cabin to the left as well as the summit of the Pico Ruivo before you continue up to the signposted fork ('PR 1.1, Ilha 7.7 km') **3** to Ilha.

Descent with views of dark green laurel-covered hillsides

If you would like to scale the Pico Ruivo, walk on past this junction; a short while later, the trail passes a third shelter. Natural stone steps then lead to a well-signposted fork in the path **4**. Here a board also provides information on the descent to Ilha (PR 1.1), while the path from Pico do Arieiro joins from the left (→ Walk 17). Keep right and, after more steps, the path soon reaches the **mountain cabin 5** with a large forecourt beneath the summit. There is also a small barbecue hut, behind which is a toilet (reasonably clean, but always short of paper).

To the left of the small grill house, a set of steps leads further uphill. After a few minutes, you reach a signposted fork in the path. Turn sharply to the left, beyond which is a branch (paved and with steps) up to the summit. The path climbs quickly through a series of tight bends to the summit of **Pico Ruivo 6**, which boasts magnificent panoramic views.

If you wish to make the descent to Ilha, follow the same path back down to the signposted fork **3**, leave the mountain path and head north. ▶

Length/walking time: approx. 12.1 km, 5:20 hrs.

Terrain: this climb is the easiest way to scale the Pico Ruivo. The descent to Ilha leads down a steep ridge, and the path often features steps. A few slippery sections aside, the route poses no major difficulties – though your knees will certainly feel the descent.

Marking: signs and red-yellow stripes. The path's official name is 'PR 1.1, Vereda da Ilha'.

Equipment: sturdy walking shoes, sun and rain protection, warm clothing.

Supplies: take water and provisions; spring at 2. The mountain cabin 5 below the summit of Pico Ruivo is open all year round, but only sells drinks and packaged snacks (the state-owned mountain cabin was privatised and closed. In 2018, we still have no information about its reopening); Bar Parada at 19 in Ilha, basic.

Getting there: by rental car or taxi from Santana to Achada do Teixeira. The (signposted) turnoff is on the old ER 101 to the southeast of the centre of Santana at the Repsol petrol station. The road from Pico das Pedras onward is only open from 7am to 9pm.

Getting back: by taxi or with the owner of Bar Parada back to Achada do Teixeira or Santana. The owner does not have a taxi licence, but sometimes offers to make the journey (about €25). If not, you can at least order a taxi in the bar (mobile ✆ 963-729375). Taxi stand in Santana, ✆ 291-572540; Bus → p. 28.

Walk 16

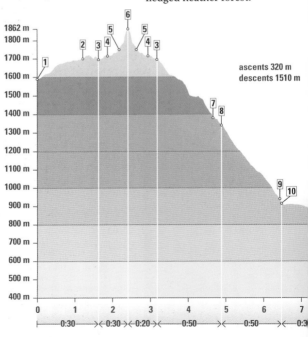

► The path runs diagonally across the hillside, and a red-yellow paint mark can be seen on a rock. After crossing this steep side valley, a short passage made safe by wire cable railings follows. Continue diagonally down a meadow slope until you come to a rocky ridge covered in tree heath and heather bushes. Newly laid steps help you negotiate steeper sections, and the path crosses an old, weathered patch of scree before briefly climbing beyond a bare saddle.

However, the descent soon steepens again. Steps supported by wooden struts have been cut into the soft tuff. As the path descends, the heather bushes increasingly turn into a fully-fledged heather forest.

A carefully laid path

ascents 320 m
descents 1510 m

In a right-hand hairpin bend, an overgrown path **7** forks off to the left. There's still a signpost for 'Semagral' here – although it's hardly accessible these days – in any case, walk past it and continue downwards.

A few minutes later, another narrow path **8** branches off to the left on a right-hand bend. To help you orientate yourself, look out for a single, isolated pine tree and steps with wooden supports which start again shortly after the fork. A few steps later, the path leads to some boulders from where there are striking views into the steep valley heads: these form the headwaters of the Ribeira de São Jorge, which opens into the sea at Calhau de São Jorge (→ Walk 12).

The path with steps then continues down. The first signs of laurel forest vegetation appear in the form of young lily-of-the-valley trees (→ p. 18), and the tree heath and heather bushes become

> **Detour from** 10: If part of the marked path is impassable or too dangerous, you're better off returning to the first fork 9 towards Vale da Lapa lodge. At the fork, coming up from below, keep right and climb slightly. The old cobbled path is hardly used and is becoming overgrown – repairs are long overdue. As it continues, the path crosses the hillside on a more or less level course. Rising gently, it leads past the deserted **Vale da Lapa lodge**; beyond it, a meadow invites walkers to take a breather. The cobbled path continues to descend beyond the lodge, though the cobbles soon disappear. A rocky, loamy section then leads through a narrow pass, and quickly reaches the fork 12 where the path meets the official PR 1.1 route.

increasingly interspersed by laurel trees and large ferns as the descent continues. Above an altitude of about 1,000 m, the **laurel forest** (→ p. 16) becomes the predominant form of vegetation.

The route downhill becomes an old cobbled path as it traverses the laurel forest. At a fork **9**, it leads straight on to the Vale da Lapa lodge (signposted). However, the official, marked PR 1.1 route to Ilha branches off to the right before steps supported by wooden struts lead through several bends to another fork **10**. Taking a few steps to the right leads to the Levada do Caldeirão Verde (→ Walk 13 and variants 3 and 4 of this route). However, your route bears left towards Ilha (signposted, '3.8 km').

Shortly after, you reach another old levada. Nowadays, it no longer serves as a water channel and merely functions as a footpath, which you follow. Some sections along the vertical wall are reinforced with new wire cable railings while vegetation provides protection in ▶

▶ others. In any case, tread carefully in these sections. (If the railings have slipped downhill or are in poor condition – which can occur as a result of heavy rain and brittle rock – then I would advise against following this route, and would instead recommend the **detour**; → Box p. 97).

A path **11** joins from the left, but you continue straight on. Immediately afterwards, steps branch off and climb upwards, but your route ignores these and continues on to another fork **12**. The path from the Vale da Lapa lodge joins from the left (weatherworn signpost). You continue straight downhill to Ilha via the now familiar steps with wooden support struts.

Variants 1, 2, 3 and 4

✳ From Achada do Teixeira, up Pico Ruivo and back via the same path. Many walkers enjoy the simplest and very popular variant of this route. It is also the easiest way to scale the island's highest peak and enjoy magnificent views without risks. Good paths, while the last stretch from the mountain cabin to the summit runs along a rocky path. Walking time 2 hrs.

✳✳✳ From Achada do Teixeira, up Pico Ruivo, and from there as per Walk 17 (in reverse) to Pico do Arieiro. No public transport routes serve Pico do Arieiro. The closest taxi rank is in Camacha, ✆ 291-922185. Walking time about 4 hrs.

✳✳✳ From 10 along the Levada do Caldeirão Verde to Queimadas (→ Walk 13: from 6 onwards in reverse). Walking time from 10 to Queimadas is a good 1 hr. Taxi rank in Santana, ✆ 291-572540.

✳✳✳ From 10, detour along the Levada do Caldeirão Verde into the Caldeirão Verde (→ Walk 13, from 7 to 11, and then back) and on to Ilha. Additional walking time for the detour about 2 hrs, out and back.

Reforested eucalyptus trees soon eclipse the native vegetation. The narrow path leads down a wide, loamy track that is overgrown with grass and moss in places **13**. This track is lined by hydrangeas, while numerous lily-of-the-valley trees (→ p. 18) grow on the hillsides; the gradient reduces here, and your knees will be grateful for it!

The path then forks off to the left **14** in a right-hand bend. Steps lead down to a narrow meadow path which runs over a ridge with a moderate gradient, though the path soon becomes steeper once again. Some tuff steps, which are slippery in parts, lead through a dark pass and soon come to a road **15** once more. The marked path continues directly opposite but, in light of my experiences with the rather enclosed, slippery pass, I would opt for the leisurely and somewhat extended version with better views, and continue to descend by following the road. There are signs for Ermida, a district of Ilha. The track you left at 14 soon joins from the right **16**, as you continue down to the left.

Slightly further on, another overgrown track joins the path, but you stay on the main path and soon reach fields where lemon trees grow. The track then comes to a road **17** leading up from Ilha and bending into the valley to the right. Here, carry on straight ahead. The official path then joins immediately from the left. At the entrance (or rather exit), a board **18** provides information about the route you have travelled.

The tarmac road then takes you past **Miradouro do Cabeço do Resto**. Your route does not deviate from this street again, and follows a few bends through the upper part of the village to the **church 19** of **Ilha** and the rather futuristic municipal centre. On the left-hand side of the street is Bar Parada with its mini-supermarket which, in good weather, has tables and chairs outside. ▪

**** The King's Route from Pico do Arieiro and up the Pico Ruivo

This walk leads through the most extraordinary section of Madeira's mountain landscape, with steep sides and distinctive peaks lining the route. Early in the year, walkers can find the endemic Madeira yellow violet with its curious blooms, while branching orchids are particularly common in early summer. For all lovers of rugged mountainous landscapes, this route will without doubt be one of the highlights, if not the highlight, of the walking holiday!

There are two different routes from Pico do Arieiro to Pico Ruivo: the somewhat shorter western route, and the eastern route across a slope of the island's second highest peak, 'Pico das Torres'. Madeira's high mountainous region is regularly subject to rockfalls and mudslides. As a result, one of the two routes is often closed off, and so for this edition I will describe the **western route as the main route** (the eastern route is shown on the map as a dotted line; the route description is in the box further below and the GPS data is given as the return route).

If both variants are walkable, feel free to combine the two. For the **complete round trip**, you should allow for a 6 to 7 hour walk with breaks. Both routes can also be followed in reverse using my directions. You can find reliable information on which routes are walkable at www.visitmadeira.pt under 'USEFUL INFO'. The starting point is the large car park directly below the summit of **Pico do Arieiro**, where

Protected path amongst the peaks

a modern building houses a visitor centre and a bar. From the car park ▋1 a set of steps leads directly up to the peak of Madeira's third highest mountain. The summit marker ▋2 is also reached in a matter of minutes, and provides magnificent views of Madeira's mountainous region and of a NATO radar station.

The path branches off just below the summit (towards the car park). It is signposted 'PR 1 Pico Ruivo, E, 7 km' and 'Pico Ruivo, O, 5.6 km'. **Note:** The 'E' stands for east (Port.: este). The 'O' stands for west (Port.: oeste) – your route.

The path, paved with basalt and trachyte slabs, starts off down over a ridge exposed to the wind, and then undulates gently before reaching a T-junction ▋3. Turn off to the right at this point and, shortly after, there is an outlook point where you can get a good overview over parts of the route.

This outlook point is called **Mira-douro do Ninho da Manta** (the buzzard's nest). Returning from this viewpoint, your route continues straight on and up over a natural stone stairway, before the gently undulating path leads far above the side valley of **Curral das Freiras** (→ Walks 18, 19 and 20). Two narrow ridges then follow, but the path over both is well protected.

A second viewpoint ▋4 with a table carved into the tuff again provides spectacular vistas.

After this viewpoint, the path once again undulates slightly along the sheer rock face, but was carefully constructed and is well secured. Soon afterwards, steep rising steps must be negotiated. After passing a rounded rock arch, the path comes to a tunnel entrance ▋5.

The well paved tunnel leads through the **Pico do Gato** (Eng.: roughly translates to 'cat's back'), and doesn't take long to go through so you don't need a ▶

Length/walking time: western route, one-way, approx. 5.3 km, 2:30 hrs. Allow the same time for the return journey.

Terrain: both routes (eastern and western) run along well-laid rocky mountain paths which feature coarse gravel in places. Various rocky and metal steps must be negotiated, which means the route is relatively demanding, and it is hard to find a steady pace. Passages over exposed sections or against rock faces are well protected with wire cable railings. If railings or safety devices are in poor condition, take a different route! I would advise against the route entirely in case of rain or strong winds – **risk of rockfalls!** In **snowy conditions** (possible from December to April), nobody should so much as attempt this route, as the rock steps are covered with sheer ice.

Marking: red-yellow stripes in places. In any case, the route is clear and has the official designation PR 1.

Supplies: take appropriate amounts of supplies and water for the route length. Bar opposite the visitor centre by the car park ▋1 offers snacks (daily, approx. 9am–7pm). The mountain cabin ▋11 was privatised and closed in 2017. I will provide updates on www.michael-mueller-verlag.de.

Getting there: by car, drive over the Poiso pass to Pico do Arieiro; signposted. No bus connection. Taxi rank in Camacha ✆ 291-922185.

Walk 17

▶ torch. At the end, steps once again lead upwards. After an extremely steep set of natural stone steps, you come to a fork in the path **6**. (To the right, the eastern route also leads to Pico Ruivo but, before research for this 4th edition of the book, it was blocked by a landslide; → Box 'Eastern route across the slopes of Pico das Torres'.)

For the western route, keep left. The path then continues past two rock shelters without any significant change in altitude before a spectacular section along the near-vertical western face of Pico das Torres. Far below to the left are the upper ridges of the Nun's Valley (Curral das Freiras).

The following tunnel is rather longer and bends so that, for the first few metres, you can't see the other side. Shortly after, the route enters the next tunnel, which is about 200m long.

Then, after three more short tunnels, there is a short climb and descent which leads to a wide outcrop **7** – a good spot for a short break before the subsequent summit attempt.

Walking under an overhanging cliff, you soon come to a fork **8**. (Climbing straight on, there is a path through a 20m long tunnel on the eastern route back to the starting point – but only if it has been unblocked.) For the climb to Pico Ruivo, turn left here and head downhill.

At first, head down some rocky steps (heading west). After a short, flat section, you come to the first of the route's five steep, demanding sets of metal steps. The last set is the steepest. It leads into a gully with steps cut into it and, after a few winding sections, the route leads to a small saddle from where you descend sharply down rocky steps.

After a few minutes' descent, you come to a fork **9** and the terrain becomes less demanding. Your route continues to the left below a sort of balcony in the rock face. (The eastern route then joins from the right, but has recently suffered severe damage.)

The route then rises gently as it passes by knotted old tree heath bushes, some of which are said to be 300 years old. Many of their species fell victim to the fire of 2010. However, most of the roots survived and have slowly begun to sprout again.

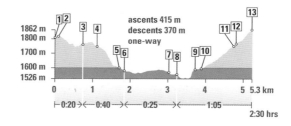

A sharp left-hand bend **10** provides a lovely view of the island's mountainous region. The path then leads through long bends – some with steps and some paved – up the mountain.

Then, directly ahead, is a fork **11** in the path. Here, you could bear right towards 'Achada do Teixeira' (signposted) and Ilha (→ Walk 16 and Variant 2 of that route). However, the destination of this route is Pico Ruivo.

To reach this peak, climb the steps to the left until you reach the area in front of the **mountain cabin 12**; there is also a small barbecue hut with a toilet to the rear (always short of paper, but reasonably clean). ▶

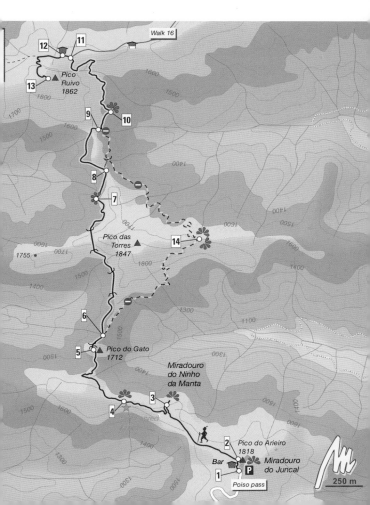

Past jagged outcrops

▶ Past the small barbecue hut, a set of steps leads further uphill. A few minutes later, the route comes to a signposted fork in the road. Turn sharply to the left, and follow the final climb (paved, with steps). The route climbs steeply through tight bends to the **summit of Pico Ruivo 13**. Then return to the start via the same route. ■

Eastern route across the slopes of Pico das Torres

Length/walking time: approx. 7 km, 3 hrs. This variant was closed in 2017, so be sure to check the current situation.

Terrain: the eastern route is more demanding, as it involves an additional climb and descent.

Directions: At the fork in the path 6 the eastern route leads off to the right, undulating gently at first before rising sharply up natural stone steps. As soon as you've negotiated the first set, the next follows, with the last set being the steepest. The steps are all different heights, which makes it difficult to get into a steady rhythm – happily, though, a fairly flat section follows and allows you to recover.

Despite the demanding terrain, the route reaches the saddle 14 on the eastern face of Pico das Torres quite quickly. This is a good spot to take a break and look back on the route walked so far. Beyond the saddle, the route winds back and forth, descending down steps in parts. A paved route then leads through a scree field featuring phonolite (sound stones; → p. 13), a light-coloured rock that clatters like pieces of glass and makes many different sounds. The flattest, thinnest rocks sound the best.

After the **field of phonolite**, the descent levels out and is well protected as it leads through a sheer rock face. You then have to climb a very short section until the route descends to a tunnel entrance to the left. The 20m long tunnel must be negotiated. The original onward path avoided it but, in 2013, a severe landslide completely tore the path away and, even in 2017, no repairs had been planned.

After traversing the tunnel, a short climb follows to a junction 9 where the eastern and western routes meet.

The village of Curral das Freiras was only connected to the island's road network in the 1950s. Previously, when its residents had wanted to leave the 'Nuns' Valley', they took this route.

✶✶ From the Eira do Serrado viewpoint to Curral das Freiras

▶▶ The starting point is the car park **1** at **Eira do Serrado** with a hotel, souvenir shop, bar and restaurant. At the entrance to the car park is a sign for 'Eira do Serrado 1094 m', beyond which concrete steps lead up to the old connection to Curral das Freiras.

First of all, however, it's worth making a detour to the viewpoint itself. To do so, walk past the vast hotel complex to a sign on the left-hand side ('Miradouro'), where a path paved with concrete slabs climbs gently. Some steps then follow and lead up to the utterly spectacular **viewpoint** at **Eira do Serrado 2**.

The cliff below plummets hundreds of metres vertically downwards. Then head back to the car park **1** via the same route.

At the sign for 'Eira do Serrado 1094 m', climb down the concrete steps to the old cobbled path leading further downwards through a chestnut forest just below the hotel complex. A short while later, the path flattens out and crosses the hillside, twisting back and forth as it descends.

The old regional road ER 107 soon comes into view. From the 1950s until 2004, this was the only road to Curral das Freiras. Then, a tunnel was opened that ▶

Length/walking time: approx. 2.8 km, 1:10 hrs.
Terrain: route along a relatively well-maintained cobbled path. **Surefootedness** is required as the paving can be very slippery when wet. Children always enjoy ice cream and cake at the end of the route, as well as the fun bus ride home.
Marking: none.
Equipment: sturdy walking shoes, sun and rain protection.
Supplies: at the Hotel Estalagem Eira do Serrado with its large souvenir shop, bar, restaurant and pleasant outdoor seating, ✆ 291/710060, www.eiradoserrado. com. Curral das Freiras features numerous bars and restaurants.
Tip: a lovely and relatively tranquil spot is the Restaurant Sabores do Curral, directly across from the bus stop, ✆ 291-712257. Quick, friendly service. Typical island dishes and, of course, chestnut-based specialities from the valley.
Getting there: by taxi or car, take the ER 107 towards Curral das Freiras; turn off to the left to Eira do Serrado (signposted) before the tunnel. Large car park at Eira do Serrado.
Getting back: good bus connections → p. 28.

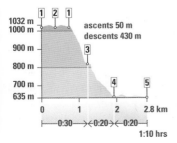

Walk 18

Beautiful view into the Nuns' Valley

▶ avoided the precipitous sections and, shortly afterwards, the old road was closed due to the risk of rockfall.

The cobbled path runs very close to the old road, but never actually meets it. After a few winding bends your route crosses a scree field, beyond which the descent becomes more slippery. The path approaches an outcrop with concrete electricity pylons.

At the outcrop, a narrow path **3** branches off and down to the left. The mini-detour is worthwhile: the outcrop provides clear views into the rugged basin of Curral das Freiras.

Soon after the outcrop, the path dives into a chestnut forest once again.

There is a very short climb before reaching a sparse eucalyptus forest **4**, though the path soon descends once again and leads past the first tiny fields that are all ploughed by hand. A set of carefully laid stone steps then leads down to the village street. Keep right and, after a few bends, you soon reach the Restaurant Sabores do Curral, with the bus stop **5** just opposite. ■

A classic route into the scenic Nuns' Valley. The houses in the locality of Curral das Freiras are spread across the entire

✳✳✳ From Corticeiras via the Boca dos Namorados to Curral das Freiras

valley basin. Centuries ago, the nuns of the Santa Clara Convent – who would later give the valley its name – fled from Funchal during a pirate attack and into the valley which, at the time, was inaccessible and home only to livestock herdsmen.

▶▶ The starting point is the bus stop **1** on the Estrada Municipal do Marco e Fonte da Pedra in Corticeiras. From there, follow this Estrada Municipal towards the Miradouro Boca dos Namorados (signposted). A few steps further, the Estrada branches off and up to the left. At this point, keep right and continue more or less straight up on.

Follow this road uphill until it bends to the left and meets the Gasse Velho da Boca dos Namorados **2**, which crosses your route. (The grounds of the Quinta Mis Muchachos can be seen to the right.) Here, you climb up to a riding stable (signposted: 'Centro hípico'). The route up to this point has been recently paved, but this surface ends on approaching the equestrian centre **3**. The old path then ascends next to the fence through the eucalyptus forest. Forestry workers are always cutting new aisles and tracks through the forest, but you shouldn't let these confuse you – the old cobbled path (which is missing its cobbles in places) continues more or less straight up through the forest.

Rather abruptly, some steps lead up to the **Boca dos Namorados** viewpoint **4**. This miradouro provides magnificent views into the rugged cauldron of Curral das Freiras.

Cross the newly paved viewpoint by heading straight along the solid wooden railings, at the end of which is the start **5** of the path to Curral das Freiras. Unfortunately, the initial section has been used as a toilet by some visitors to the viewpoint.

At first, the path descends gently down the slope, though landslides often obscure the path.

There then follows a narrower section where rocks protrude unpleasantly into the path at chest height. After this rather ▶

Length/walking time: approx. 7.8 km, 4:10 hrs.

Terrain: the descents are slippery and full of rubble. Paths across hillsides may be buried under landslips; narrow in places with plunging views. **Surefootedness and an eye for trail conditions** are necessary.

Marking: none.

Equipment: sturdy walking shoes, sun protection due to some long sections without shade.

Supplies: take drinking water and supplies. Curral das Freiras has numerous places to grab a snack, as well as this author's favourite 'end of the route bar' (→ Tip, Route 18): Sabores do Curral.

Getting there: the entire route can only be completed using public transport or a combination of rental car, bus and taxi. The bus connections, however, are good (→ p. 28).

Walk 19

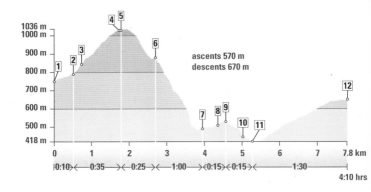

ascents 570 m
descents 670 m

▶ slippery slope crossing, the path descends more steeply, passing several chestnut trees and winding back and forth. Several slippery or overgrown passages may then follow. It might be worth taking a first break at the following outcrop, which features an electricity pylon **6**.

The beaten track which leads to the right of the outcrop is the wrong one! The correct path downhill bends to the left and winds down. It is

View into the Nuns' Valley

narrow and steep, but is generally in fairly good condition. After a demanding descent, there follows a short, almost flat section where you can recover, until mixed woodland comprising chestnut, laurel and eucalyptus trees sees the now slippery path descend more steeply once again.

Just before the first houses of Lombo Chão, the path crosses a small valley floor, from where a concrete footpath sitting atop a water pipe rises gently upwards. At the first houses, concrete steps climb up to the road to the left (be sure not to carry straight on). At the Estrada do Lombo Chão road **7** is the final bus stop of bus line 81; if you don't want to walk further, wait here for the bus.

From here, the walk continues through the lower parts of Curral das Freiras and continues along the road for a short section. It leads into a steep side valley and then begins to climb.

The Estrada Mun. da Serra Velha de Baixo **8** then branches off in a left-hand bend, but you continue to climb past this and the subsequent school (high fence around the playground). Around 40 m further on, a stepped concrete path **9** with street lights branches off to the right at a building resembling a garage. Taking this path allows you to cut off some bends in the road.

We then descend on rounded concrete steps. Stairways repeatedly branch off from yours, but can all be ignored; stay on the main path as it passes by some houses. Your path leads through a side valley of willow trees and giant canes. Just after the valley floor, a rising set of stairs branches off from the path, as does a second at a house. The street lights lining the steps might tempt you to climb them, but you're better off sticking to the main path as the steps only lead back up to the road. Long, extended concrete steps descend gently, before becoming steeper at a chestnut plantation.

Shortly before you reach the road, it becomes clear that the current concrete path is an old cobbled path.

Turn right at the road **10** and head downhill. The main valley of Curral das Freiras runs below to ▶

Shorter Version

Take a taxi from Estreito de Câmara de Lobos to the Boca dos Namorados ④. This shortens the walking time by 45 minutes.

▶ the right, but the road first leads over a side valley. You pass another bus shelter by a concrete square **11**, and continue to follow the street downhill and through the main valley.

The ascent to the **centre of Curral das Freiras** then begins and, shortly before you reach your destination, the road flattens out and soon comes to the **Sabores do Curral** restaurant. The bus stop **12** for services to Funchal is directly opposite. ■

Demanding and often isolated walk over Madeira's main ridge, where the billowing fog and the dark-green of the laurel and heath tree forest creates an other-worldly atmosphere.

✱✱✱✱ From Curral das Freiras over the main ridge to the Encumeada pass

▶ ▶ The starting point is located on the road from Curral das Freiras in the district of Fajã dos Cardos, 900 m after a road bridge on the right-hand side towards 'Pico do Furão' (don't bear left towards Fajã Escura). Leave the road in **Fajã dos Cardos** via some concrete steps and join the Vereda da Fajã do Capitão **1**. After a short distance, turn off the village road to the left and cross a stone bridge over the river that bears the route's first red-yellow marking .

After the bridge, an old cobbled path leads upwards and crosses a levada straight away. At a subsequent fork **2** in the path, continue to the left along level ground where a natural stone wall bears faded markings.

Then walk past small, painstakingly cultivated terraced fields, cross another levada and climb into the eucalyptus forest. The red-yellow marking is a regular sight on the route. A small clearing **3** provides further scenic views of the steep slopes of the Curral das Freiras. The narrow path leading sharply uphill at this point only serves to cut off one bend in the main route. Follow the winding route for a longer period through the eucalyptus forest, almost all of which was severely affected by the 2010 forest fire.

After the forest has thinned out a little, the path leads over a slope with gorse bushes (that have become ▶

Length/walking time: approx. 8.3 km, 4:50 hrs.

Terrain: demanding mountain hike with numerous climbs and often slippery descents. The main ridge is often shrouded in fog. Conditions along the walk vary from very warm to humid-cold and windy on the main ridge: even if you set off in blazing sunshine, you must be prepared for poor weather on the route. Some exposed passages are protected; the unsecured sections should pose no problems for experienced mountaineers. Though other walkers are rarely encountered, occasional walking groups traverse the main ridge.

Marking: red-yellow stripes.

Equipment: sturdy walking shoes, sun and rain protection, warm clothing.

Supplies: take food and **drinks**, and **plenty** of them. At the end of the walk **14** is Bar-Restaurante Encumeada, directly by the pass, ✆ 291-952319.

Getting there: by taxi or car, take regional road ER 107 to Curral das Freiras. In Curral das Freiras, head towards the district of Fajã Escura (signposted). The road leads through two tunnels. 1.5 km after the first tunnel, turn right at a bridge towards Pico do Furão. 900 m after the bridge, between two groups of houses, the Vereda da Fajã Capitão branches off into the valley floor. Bus → p. 29.

Getting back: take a taxi to Ribeira Brava (town taxi rank ✆ 291-951800), from where there are numerous connections to Funchal and the west of the island. Bus → p. 29.

Walk 20

►somewhat overgrown). Beyond this, the eucalyptus forest becomes thicker once again.

As you climb higher, tree heath bushes become increasingly common among the eucalyptus trees. A few metres beyond the last eucalyptus trees, the path forks. Bear left **4** and then, a few steps later, the red-yellow marking can be seen on a rock. By this point, tree heath bushes have entirely supplanted the eucalyptus trees. A slope crossing then follows and features striking views of the mountain backdrop. Walking up the following zigzagging path, it becomes evident that it is an old cobbled road – even at this altitude.

After a relatively sharp incline, the path finally reaches the **Torrinha pass 5**, where several signs point in various directions. (The path to the right, heading east, leads to the Pico Ruivo – 5.1 km, about 2:15 hrs – and on to Pico do Arieiro – 11.4 km, about 5 hrs; the route to the north descends to Boaventura. However, this path, overgrown and in poor condition, is seldom used and not recommended.)

The destination of this route – the Encumeada pass – is signposted to the west. From the pass, continue to climb – after a breather, of course – heading west up steep natural stone steps. Wire cable

Tip

If you're arriving by car, you'll need to collect your vehicle after the walk – rental cars are not safe if left here overnight. For evening buses, see→ p. 29.

ascents 960 m
descents 670 m

0:40 ✕ 1:40 ✕

Through green valleys

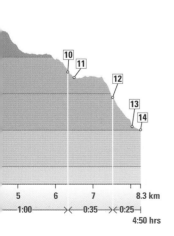

railings secure steep and sloping sections.

After the steps, the path continues more or less level over the more humid northern side, which often features clouds of mist. However, the path soon climbs once again; you switch back to the south side and walk through a dense tree heath forest. Steps then lead up to a jagged crevice **6**.

Beyond it, you switch back to the northern side, where steep steps lead downhill. Although the slope to the right falls away sharply, it is overgrown and the path is very wide with wire cable railings in some sections. After the steps, ▶

▶ another short slope crossing follows before the final significant ascent begins: climb up a dirt path permeated by rocks and steps, and continue past an alcove **7** cut into the tuff rock, which once served as a shelter for shepherds.

After climbing some more steps, reach a rocky ridge and, further up, gain a clear view of the south coast. You walk along this ridge, more or less without a set path, but always climbing gently. There are sheer drops to the left and right, but both slopes are overgrown. A series of cairns help to show the way. After the ridge, the path becomes clear once again, and it's not long before you encounter more red-yellow markings.

At an altitude of 1,630m, finding your way across this open, reddish tuff section **8** can prove difficult in foggy conditions. However, if you continue straight over it for a few paces, you soon come to a clear path that leads gently downhill.

It's then a pleasant stroll on the central ridge through fairytale-like heather shrubland followed by a longer downhill section on the northern side.

High over Ribeira Brava

After a descent with steps, a clearing and fire pit **9** to the right of the path offers an ideal spot for a well-earned break.

The path pivots back onto the southern side shortly after the clearing, and you continue downhill through tree heath bushes where the path is rocky, earthy and full of steps.

Some slippery rocks must be negotiated in a humid valley, but difficult sections are made safer with wire cable railings. ▶

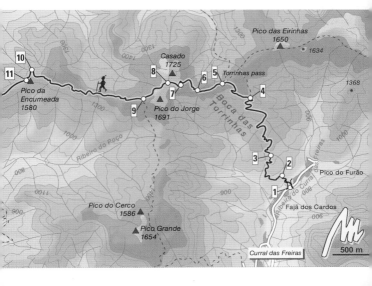

Jagged mountains in the valley of Curral das Freiras

▶ The path then takes a sharp right-hand bend above a rock arch. In good conditions, the wind turbines on the Paúl da Serra plateau can be seen from here. There then follows a section beneath a sheer trachyte (→ p. 13) rock face. Flora on the hillside includes lily-of-the-valley trees and some lovely specimens of the knotted Madeira laurel tree (→ p. 16) covered with ferns, moss and sedums.

Beyond an old goats' gate, there is a hillside covered in ferns and gorse bushes with a clear view of the wide valley of Ribeira Brava. The path then leads beneath another steep rock face. After undulating for a brief time, the path bends to the right and back onto the northern side, where a usually slippery and damp section follows. Steep natural stone steps lead down to an alcove **10** – another spot for a short breather before the final descent.

The path becomes extremely slippery after the alcove, particularly in a section involving natural stone steps. You switch back to the south side and go down steep steps **11** secured with wire cable railings. A pleasantly flat section then follows along the middle of the main ridge

(with tree heath bushes to the left and right), but steps soon ascend once again. Above, a mountain – the Pico da Encumeada – temporarily shields you from the northerly wind.

The steep descent to the Encumeada pass then begins slowly as steps alternate with more even sections. The path bends one final time to the northern side, where it remains until reaching the Encumeada pass. More natural stone steps then have to be negotiated.

One of the specially designed sets of steps 12 is particularly steep with exceptionally narrow stepping areas.

Caution: some of the steps wobble, so tread carefully and use the railings! With a little caution, though, these steps are soon crossed. Concentration is also required for the steps and stairs that follow.

The pass and its transmission masts then come into view quite suddenly. At the end of the footpath, a board 13 provides information on the entire ridge path. (The route from Achada do Teixeira is extremely difficult to organise for individual walkers.)

From the board, a stony track leads down to the pass road 14 over Encumeada pass. To the right, it continues to São Vicente; heading straight on leads to the Paúl da Serra plateau, while turning left and around the corner leads towards Ribeira Brava.

Walk down the road towards Ribeira Brava which, a short distance later leads to **Bar Encumeada**. Directly opposite is the bus stop for journeys to Ribeira Brava. ∎

**** From the Boca da Corrida over the Pico Grande into the Nuns' Valley

This varied mountain walk provides magnificent views into the Ribeira Brava valley and across to Curral das Freiras. The demanding Pico Grande offers one of Madeira's most sublime summit experiences for proficient mountaineers.

▶▶ The starting point is the small car park **1** by the Boca da Corrida viewpoint below the **Pico da Malhada**. The car park features a holy shrine dedicated to São Cristóvão (St. Christopher). To the left of this, a narrow cobbled road leads further up to an information board that offers details about the course of the official route PR 12 to the Encumeada pass (→ Box p. 120). The walk itself starts at a path with natural stone steps that lead up beside the information board.

A wooden sign points the way ('PR 12, Encumeada 12.6 km'). At first, the path climbs quite sharply, although this first steep section is crossed in about 10 minutes and an outcrop **2** offers the chance to catch your breath. From here, there is a wonderful view of the island's highest peaks, Curral das Freiras and right down to Funchal.

The strange, rugged mountain of the Pico Grande

The route then continues to climb, though less steeply, up a path paved with stones. The paving ends a few metres later; the path then levels out and even descends for a short time. The slope to the right falls away sharply towards Curral das Freiras (Nuns' Valley). You might feel a little dizzy here, but the path here is very wide.

The path then bends sharply down to the left at another outcrop **3** and gives an initial view of the Encumeada pass. It descends more sharply from here on; steep passages are paved with stones.

Then, where the path becomes flatter, several chestnut trees can be seen on the slope falling away to the right. There follows a small saddle, from where a path branches off sharply backwards and to the left **4**. (The path that branches off is usually so overgrown that it is barely visible, though sometimes it is also well-trodden.) Do not turn off here: this path ends with steep drops high above the Ribeira Brava valley. Your walk continues straight on from this saddle.

After a short, flat section, another climb follows up to another outcrop **5**.

The path then descends over rough stone paving to a narrow saddle; from here, the path ▶

Length/walking time: approx. 7.6 km, 4:30 hrs.

Terrain: this long-distance walk runs along stony dirt mountain paths. Surefootedness is required as a few sections feature views into the distance and far below. For the climb to the Pico Grande, **surefootedness and a head for heights** are absolute necessities. The final metres have to be climbed.

Marking: signposts and colour markings, cairns in places around the Pico Grande.

Equipment: sturdy walking shoes, sun and rain protection.

Supplies: take everything; the end of the walk features the quaint Snackbar O Lagar 14 in Fajã Escura – also a grocery shop for locals, it serves delicious skewers (Espetada) with chicken (Frango) or beef (Vaca) if you pre-order or are prepared to wait, open daily, ☎ 291-712520.

Getting there: the route is hard to reach with a car, as walking back to the start takes too long. The best option is a combination of bus and taxi: take the bus to Estreito de Câmara de Lobos (line 137 Rodoeste, 1-2x per hour, and take the taxi from there to the starting point (about €10) or take the bus (→ p. 29) the whole way; same for the return journey.

The sheer rock face beneath the Pico Grande

▶ climbs for a few minutes. It then continues more or less level across a hillside, until it descends once again down the western side of another saddle by the name of Boca do Cerro. This section is overgrown with gorse, which often protrudes into the path.

Variants

Climbing the Pico Grande represents an experience in itself. As a result, it's not the end of the world if you simply return on the same path from 1 to 11 (out/return 4 hrs). Of course, you can also walk down into the Nuns' Valley 'without the peak': this route is also enjoyable and saves climbing and descending the Pico Grande.

If you want to walk on to the Encumeada pass, don't branch off at the Boca do Cerro at 6: simply continue straight on. Though landslides had long rendered this path inaccessible, it has recently been restored and re-opened. It ends at the pass road beneath the Encumeada pass, which, 10 minutes later, leads down to the Hotel Residencial Encumeada. Rodoeste bus line 6 from Ribeira Brava to Funchal departs here (between 3.30pm and 4pm).

When you've almost walked down the side of the saddle, a narrow path 6 branches off to the right. A cairn, a sign for 'Relvinha' and four natural stone steps mark its start. This is where you leave the official route PR 12.

You then walk a short stretch up to the saddle. At the top, bear left (large sign: 'Pico') and climb another short stretch to a

meadow with a fire pit and some distinctive chestnut trees.

Cross the meadow to the left, where 'Pico Grande' has been painted on a stone. You pass by a nook in the rock, and a steep and exposed ascent then follows. A wire cable secured in the wall helps on the climb, and a wire cable railing has also been fitted. Though this rocky climb is only brief, it's still important to proceed carefully.

After this section, the path comes to an outcrop **7**. From there, the next short section ascends only slightly, but the next steps and rock climbs soon follow. The subsequent ascent is well marked by cairns, and the path here is well-trodden.

Your route, the direct path to the summit, bends up to the left at an inconspicuous fork **8**. (Following the 'old path' would lead you straight on at this point and up to the peak through a long bend. However, this variant is rarely used.)

You then climb steeply up to a rocky ledge, where you bear right and walk over bare rock for some 20m. At the end of this rock formation, **9** climb sharply once again up to the left. A few bends later, the 'old path' comes up from the right to join yours **10**. Here, continue ▶

Walking down old roads

At one time, numerous cobbled roads crossed Madeira's mountainous landscape. Nature later reclaimed these areas so that, today, only narrow footpaths remain and serve as a boon for walkers. Official walking path PR 12, which this route starts on, was once a key trade route that linked the northern side of the island to the south via the Encumeada pass. The northern side's terrain is very steep and the sea is often wild and rough. As a result, trade goods such as wine and agricultural produce had to be taken to the south side and loaded onto ships there. At over 1,000m, the Encumeada pass is still the lowest passage through the centre of the island, and the trade road was thus of key significance at the start of the 20th century. In those days, the cobbled path to Curral das Freiras was also considered a 'road'.

▶ heading left and uphill until the path reaches a meadow directly below the final summit section.

From here, it's an **easy scramble**: from the meadow, head straight for the summit. Climb gently to the left up a short gully. A right-hand bend then leads up to a ridge which has to be scaled. The wire cables here are not always helpful: some sections are loose and wires protrude in others, meaning you could cut your hands. The best method is just to hold on to any 'sprouting' rock. After the ridge, a left-right combination takes you along a wire cable. The last few metres up to the summit of the **Pico Grande 11** must be negotiated without cables.

Then follow the same route back down to the meadow with the striking chestnut trees. Down below on the eastern side, the easily recognisable path leads to Curral das Freiras.

The path crosses the slope with a gentle declining gradient and continues through a side valley filled with debris and scree. It's then a little climb before a series of steeper winding bends. A particularly slippery section is protected by wire cable railings. There then follows a rocky ridge **12** that requires a head for heights, as the slope to the right plummets vertically for several hundred metres. The drop to the left is a little less steep. Thankfully, railings to the left and right provide at least psychological protection.

After the ridge, a more recognisable former cobbled path leads down to the left. Slope crossings alternate with hairpin bends on the descent through the chestnut forest. The route is clear, but can be slippery when wet.

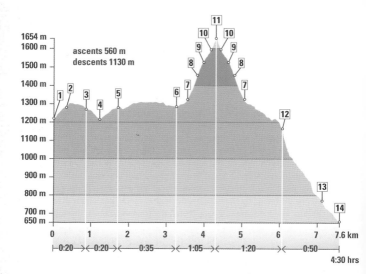

Just before the end of the route, the path fans out into several tracks through the eucalyptus forest – though it's impossible to get lost. Look out for a narrow, steep path to the right that is only a few metres long and leads to a partially concrete track **13**, where you turn and go down to the left.

The track become a village street on reaching the first houses. After a few private gardens, the **Snackbar O Lagar 14** is on the right-hand side of the road in **Fajã Escura**, and marks the end of this route. Some 20 m further down is the bus stop for journeys to Funchal (few services). A better choice is to walk a few minutes to the next bus stop on the valley road in **Colmeal**. ▪

** Circuit from Lombo do Mouro over the scenic Bica da Cana mountain

This route features diverse rural scenery and varied trail conditions. It leads past the prominent Pináculo rock formation, then heads to the 'Sugar Loaf mountain', Bica da Cana, and the plateau, before circling back to the starting point, Lombo do Mouro.

▶▶ The starting point is beside the information board **1** for official walking path **PR 17, Pináculo – Folhadal**. It is located at a right-hand bend on regional road ER 110, 3.2 km from the Encumeada pass towards Porto Moniz/Paúl (with parking available at a rough bulge in the road).

Walk some 200 m along the road from the parking bay back towards the Encumeada pass until the footpath begins at a left-hand bend. A signpost **2** points the way to Caramujo (6.4 km) and Encumeada (14 km). A few steps lead up to the levada, which resembles a stream, and you follow it to the north-east above the road. Some 5 minutes later, the path runs directly below a steep rock face where water

Duck!

continuously drips and gurgles. **Caution: slip hazard!** Next is a narrow section beneath overhanging rock where you have to balance along the levada wall, though there are railings to help on this section. Further sections have been made more easily passable with concrete, including under a lovely waterfall **3** that, thankfully, does not pour directly onto the path. This waterfall supplies the levada.

After passing a few rocks from a landslide, the path ascends gradually, and is quite easy at first – but soon there are steps up an old cobbled path through mixed woodland with tree heath and laurel trees. After a few minutes' climb, the path's course is skilfully cut into the rock face. This stretch features wide views down to Serra de Água and back up to the island's highest peaks. Railings guard the steep terrain. After passing this rock face, the path twice crosses a steep water channel cut into the rock.

The winding path then leads up some steps and directly onto the ridge. You then meet the levada **4** again by some rocks. A flat section provides a first view of the Pináculo, an ancient volcanic vent, to the right. A few steps then follow before the narrow dirt path runs more or less flat along the levada through dense tree heath woodland. The branches protrude very low into the path – **mind your head!** ▶

Length/walking time: approx. 9.3 km, 3:30 hrs.
Terrain: circular walk on mountain paths, narrow in places; restored cobbled paths in sections and along a mountain levada that looks like a stream. Some short vertiginous sections, mostly protected by railings. Inclines are short but steep.
Marking: none. The route follows official path PR 17 for a time.
Equipment: sturdy walking shoes, sun and rain protection – the route passes waterfalls.
Supplies: take drinking water, no snack points on the route.
Getting there: individually by taxi or car along the ER 110 between the Encumeada pass and Porto Moniz. 3.2 km from the pass is a board for the official PR 17 footpath: park here. Taxis in Ribeira Brava ☎ 291-951800, São Vicente ☎ 291-842238, local multilingual driver (EN, FR, IT, ES) Gilberto Andrade (mobile ☎ 963-671604, gilbertoandrade64@hotmail.com. No bus connection.

Walk 22

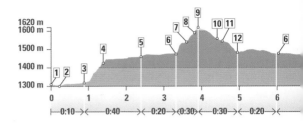

▶ After crossing a first slope, rounded steps at **5** lead below the craggy **Pináculo**. Four small natural stone walls offer a spot to rest. From here, the path is flat and leads through 2–3 m high tree heath and heather bushes before reaching a vertical rock face that the path runs beneath. Water always drips on the path here, and steep sections are protected with wire cable railings. Take the chance to gaze down

into the São Vicente valley. After an over-grown section, the path again runs along the rock face under overhanging rock and, immediately after, widens out to an open space. A mere 10 m later, a steep, narrow path **6** forks off and up to the left, rising steeply through tree heath bushes.

Leave the main path here, and climb sharply up a short set of earth and stone steps. A flat section by a boundary stone provides more wonderful views across Madeira's mountain region. After this flat stretch, the path crosses a rocky gully; look out for footprints leading up to the left directly after. The path is, however, quite clear.

After climbing along the gully, you pass a weathered metal board **7**, where a trodden path leads straight through a flat hollow. However, keep right after the metal board and continue to climb further along an almost derelict fence. The path leads more or less straight up through low gorse bushes. Two isolated heather trees are useful for orientation: walk straight towards them.

Just below the trees, a short section of gorse bushes make the path less pleasant. At this point, the fence (or at least, what's left of it) bends **8** down to the left. A path follows it down, but you continue to climb up to the right, and follow a right-hand bend around the heather trees used for orientation above. You then ascend gently across a hillside covered with ferns. Narrow paths regularly branch off to the left; ignore them and keep right. After a few short, rocky sections, pass a weather station directly below the summit of the Bica da Cana. The highest point of the **Bica da Cana** is indicated by a summit marker **9**.

From the peak, a path soon leads to a wide viewpoint with extensive vistas. A wide road leads up to the viewpoint from regional road ER 110. You walk down it and past another weather station featuring a net structure to measure the water content of the fog. Shortly after, your path comes to an old cobbled path **10** leading to the **Casa de Abrigo da Bica da Cana** shelter, the building just to the left.

Continue down the cobbled road to the right, which soon comes to the ER 110 **11**. Immediately on the right is the start of a narrow dirt path that leads you to the north and down through broom, gorse and ferns. Walk downhill to the left of a fence. The path soon widens out and, after a short descent, another fence joins from the left. Either look for a gap or use the wooden stiles provided to climb over. ▶

At the volcano

The Pináculo is an old volcanic vent (→ p. 11). The surrounding, softer tuff rock has been eroded away so much over the years that only the core of the vent, now a prominent rock chimney, is still standing.

▶Beyond the fence, the path continues to the left and descends through dense, tall Madeira blueberry and tree heath bushes (→ p. 18). This cobbled path is 150 to 200 years old, and little of the paving remains. A dirt path branches off to the right in a sharp left-hand bend – but only leads to a dead end. Follow the left-hand bend down the rock steps. After a few short, steep sections, you come to the officially marked **main track PR 17** **12**. Here, signs point towards 'Caramujo 3.1 km' and 'Encumeada 10.9 km'. To head back to the start, bear right (signposted as 'Lombo do Mouro 3.3 km').

At first, the path here is also lined by Madeira blueberry bushes. The path is stony, and small side streams and damp passages must be negotiated along the way. The levada begins abruptly beside a wet rock face. An interesting water inlet can be seen where steps cut into the tuff rock branch off to the right (by an overflow secured with railings).

A couple of minutes later, you come back to the fork **6**, where you left the main track on your ascent. Head back to the starting point **1** down the same path. ■

★★★ Variants: the entire PR 17

Walks along the officially signposted PR 17 are difficult for individual walkers to organise as it doesn't return to the starting point. To walk the entire route, walk past 6 towards 12 and – without branching off or making a detour – follow the path onwards. It generally leads downhill, becoming stony and full of scree in parts, on a wide, stony track leading from São Vicente to the plateau (without Bica da Cana about 3 hrs from the ER 110 to the track). On this track, descend for a few metres and then turn right into the mixed wood-land of tree heath and laurel trees (stone steps mark the start of the path). A few minutes later, there is a small lake to the right of the path. Further on, it undulates gently until it comes to an old levada, which you follow through some side valleys.

It then comes to a narrow ridge (wire cable railings on both sides), beyond which the path climbs sharply up steps and is crossed by another trail. This then leads onwards and climbs up to the Levada do Norte. Follow it in the direction of water flow to the southern side. Pass through two tunnels and, after the second (where the levada flows to the left of the path for the first time), keep left and walk along the wide, modern Levada Grande, which reaches the Encumeada pass in about 10 minutes. Return journey only possi-ble by taxi (approx. €15 to Ribeira Brava) or hitchhiking back to the starting point by the information board for the official PR 17 route. You should allow 5-6 hrs for the entire PR 17 circuit. Don't forget your torch.

*Along the Levada do Paúl at the edge of the Paúl da Serra plateau

Easy levada-based route above Rabaçal with views of the south-west coast and the Cristo Rei das Montanhas. Watch out, though – witches are said to have caused trouble here in the past ...

▶▶ The starting point is the large unsurfaced car park **1** by the ER 110 above Rabaçal (→ Walks 24 and 25). Cross the road and walk a short distance towards the Encumeada pass. To the south of the road is a large water basin. Between this basin and the ER 110 is a dirt path: walking east, it leads you to a small chapel. A wide levada supplied by the water basin must be crossed using wide stepping stones. Then keep left and head towards the **Nossa Senhora da Fátima** chapel. The narrow Levada do Paúl **2** runs above the chapel. Walk south-east along it in the direction of the water flow.

The levada flows along the southern slope of the plateau. In clear conditions, the views extend to some of the houses of Calheta on mountain ridges far below. After a gentle 15 minute amble, cross the road **3** leading from Arco da Calheta to the plateau.

> Note - Construction work is underway in the area of Pico da Urze. Afforestation is being carried out and a new reservoir is being built. Truck traffic and construction work can lead to disruptions along the Levada do Paúl and along the Levada do Alecrim.

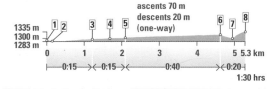

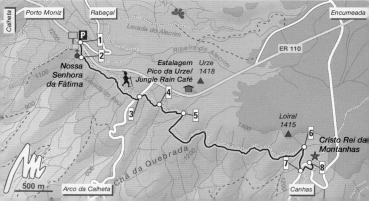

The Levada do Paúl

A little later, niches can be seen in the rock slope to the left of the levada. The path here is narrow, and walkers are forced to balance on the small levada wall for a short stretch **4**.

Even during the summer, water flows through a subsequent minor side valley **5**. After a dirt road crosses the path, the levada leads into a wide valley. The forester's lodge by the Cristo Rei das Montanhas can already be seen in the distance. The slope to the right falls away rather more sharply in this valley, though it is not dangerous. The river below generally carries water all year round.

In the final valley floor before the road, another short stretch (about 40 careful paces) must be negotiated along the narrow levada wall **6**.

A little later, the path reaches the road **7** leading from Canhas to the plateau. A large cross stands above to the left. Walk up the street, follow a long right-hand bend and, at the wall of the forester's lodge, bear left onto a stony track to the large statue of Christ. If a large herd of cows has not just occupied the area **8** beneath the **Cristo Rei das Montanhas**, this is an ideal spot for a break. Return to the starting point via the same route. ■

Length/walking time: out and return via same route, approx. 10.6 km, 3:00 hrs.

Terrain: easy levada walk with no significant change in altitude. The path becomes very narrow in some short sections along the levada. Some plunging views where slopes fall away.

Marking: none.

Equipment: sturdy walking shoes, sun and rain protection. No shade anywhere on the route!

Supplies: take water. Estalagem Pico da Urzel (also known as the Jungle Rain Café) on the plateau by regional road ER 110, rustic grill restaurant and bar adjacent: Sítio do Ovil, ✆ 291-820150, www.hotel picodaurze.com.

Getting there: individually by taxi or car along the ER 110 to the car park above Rabaçal. Taxi rank in Calheta ✆ 291-822129. No bus connection.

Walk 23

*** Along the Levada do Alecrim with a detour to the Lagoa do Vento

If you're looking for a more challenging walk in the vicinity of Rabaçal, this isolated route should suit you. It leads through secluded areas and past a lake to reach Rabaçal and then returns on a narrow road closed to traffic.

▶▶ The walk starts at the **car park 1 above Rabaçal**. First of all, follow the road to Rabaçal for a short time and pass a barrier. About 30 m beyond this, a narrow path branches off to the right by a concrete electricity pylon. Rising gently at first, it then follows a more or less level course between the ER 110 and the road leading down to Rabaçal.

After a few metres, the path widens and meets the **Levada do Alecrim 2** – a wide, modern levada which you follow for the next hour, walking against the water flow. However, the path is stony and earthy, making it easy to stumble. After about 10 minutes along the levada, the path comes to an equalising basin **3** where there are often trout to be seen. At this point, the Ribeira do Alecrim stream is channelled into the levada.

The Levada do Alecrim at 5

Watch out: the path becomes narrower from here on, and walkers must not be deceived by the vegetation that lines the steep slope for the rest of the route – if the worst comes to the worst, the bushes will not break a fall. Some 10 minutes after the equalising basin, walkers must cross a **vertigo-inducing section 4** without the apparent security of vegetation. However, this passage is only a few metres long.

Just after this, the levada flows down a steep water

slide where stone steps **5** beside it lead upwards. Although the levada narrows a little from here on, the path offers no other real difficulties apart from a few stony sections. Large bushes of the endemic Madeira blueberry (→ p. 18) then appear amongst the numerous heather bushes.

An inconspicuous fork **6** follows directly after and later leads down to the Lagoa do Vento. Look out for this fork: a narrow but obvious path joins the levada from the right and continues down to the left on the other side of the fork. At the start of the descent is a stone with a blue marking (horizontal dash above a semi-circle), though this marking can only be clearly seen from the other side, i.e. walking from the source of the levada.

Before that, however, take the **detour down to Madre**, the start (literally the 'mother') of the levada. Follow the levada to begin with; approximately 5 minutes after the fork, rocks jut into the path at shoulder and head height. The path reaches the **start of the levada 7** soon after. The idyllic spot by the stream with a small waterfall and pools to cool your feet is a perfect spot for a first break.

The path back along the levada, returns to the fork **6** in around 10 minutes, and you then take the only clearly recognisable path leading downhill. (If you're not sure, the best option is to return along the levada back to the starting point the way you came: the terrain is simply too dangerous to attempt the descent without a path or a clear sense of direction.)

The path is clear and leads down steeply through tree heath bushes. After a few steps downhill, the path comes to an outcrop with extensive views into the valley of the Ribeira da Janela stream up to the edge of the plateau.

At the outcrop, the path bends sharply down and to the left; steep rocky sections lead further ▶

Length/walking time: approx. 6.9 km and 2:15 hrs to Rabaçal **12** or 8.6 km and 2:50 hrs incl. the return route **1** via the road.

Terrain: the path along the levada is relatively straightforward, and only a short section is **exposed**. On the sharp descent, **surefootedness** and an **eye for trail conditions** are required. The path runs along the steep face in places, and is **extremely slippery** when wet!

Marking: none.

Supplies: take food and drink with you, nowhere to stop for a snack.

Getting there: the starting point is best reached by car, as there's no way to get back by bus! To the Paúl da Serra via Ribeira Brava and the Encumeada pass or via Canhas (signposted) or via Calheta (signposted). At the ER 110 from the Encumeada pass there is a large car park by the fork to Rabaçal (opposite a large water basin). The narrow access road down to the houses is blocked off. Taxi rank in Porto Moniz ✆ 291-572540, in Calheta ✆ 291-822129.

The municipality operates a shuttle service from the car park to the houses of Rabaçal (9am–7.30pm, no fixed schedule, return €5, single €3). The minibus (8 seater) runs continuously if there is sufficient demand. This allows you to skip the walk up from Rabaçal to the car park.

Walk 24

Picturesque end of the Levada do Alecrim at waypoint [7]

▶ downhill, though they are soon crossed. You then come to a levada buried by rubble, though its level course and parts of the wall are still identifiable. The way down continues some 5 m further to the right – but is now not quite as steep. After descending further, you soon come to an inconspicuous path **8** branching off to the right. Continue down to the left here; this path is also more well-trodden than the other.

Some 2 minutes later, the path crosses a small side valley where the terrain is generally very slippery. Rushing water can be heard in the distance, and you continue through a second slippery side valley – tread with caution. A third side valley then follows just 2 minutes later. The slope here is very steep, so keep to the mountain side and take care. This section is also quickly crossed.

After a section where the path is almost level, it descends sharply once again. Continue up and down for a while through tight bends until you reach another path **9** crossing yours. To the left, the blue marking is again visible on a rock, yet here the semi-circle is above the horizontal dash. The path to the left leads to the road to Rabaçal. However, the path to the right offers a **detour** to the Lagoa do Vento lake.

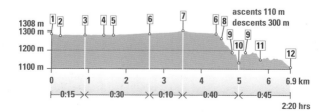

At first, the path to the right is more or less flat as it runs along the hillside. Watch out for loose rocks and stones when crossing the various narrow valleys, before the path descends once again in a series of steep winding bends. A dark green lagoon comes into sight immediately after. A few more sharp curves take you down to the **Lagoa do Vento** 🔟 beneath a sheer rock face. (Following the rocky course of the stream from the lake takes you to the steep break-off edge of the Risco waterfall; → Walk 25. Warning: this area features a vertical drop of over 100 m.)

Then follow the same route back to the fork 🟪9. From here, follow the path straight on, initially descending for a short section before climbing again and then undulating along the hillside. When crossing this slope to meet the road, **concentration is essential**: though the edge of the path may be overgrown, the vegetation disguises the fact that the slope beneath falls away **vertically in places**.

A narrow, inconspicuous path 🟪11 branching off in a sharp right-hand turn only serves to confuse matters: simply continue straight ahead.

Some 45 minutes after the Lagoa do Vento lake, you reach the narrow road 🟪12 to Rabaçal. (To the left, it leads to the car park at the starting point 🟪1 in about 30 minutes.) Or, head right and walk about 5 minutes down to the end of the road and travel back with the shuttle bus (→ Walk 25; €3). ∎

Note - Construction work is underway in the area of Pico da Urze. Afforestation is being carried out and a new reservoir is being built. Truck traffic and construction work can lead to disruptions along the Levada do Paúl and along the Levada do Alecrim.

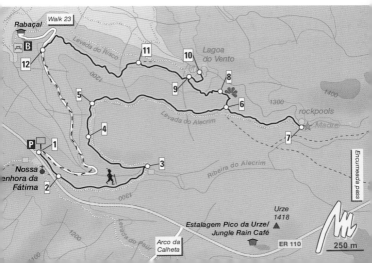

** To the Risco water-fall and the 25 springs near Rabaçal

The 25 springs – known in Portuguese as Vinte e Cino Fontes – and the Risco waterfall are particular highlights for walkers on Madeira. Children love this walk: wild and romantic forest with water gurgling and splashing everywhere. As early as the 19th century, the water – which actually flows to the north – was channelled here to the south side of the island.

▶▶ The starting point is the large **unsurfaced car park above Rabaçal**. At the start of the narrow road that leads to the houses in Rabaçal is an information board **1** describing the path's route. Signs point down the road. Walk down this road and, after only a few paces, pass through a gate. After almost 10 minutes, the road crosses the small valley floor **2** of the Ribeira do Alecrim river.

It ends directly above the houses of **Rabaçal 3**, where two signposted routes – PR 6 ('25 Fontes, 2.5 km') and PR 6.1 ('Risco, 1.2 km') branch off to the right. A path paved with rough stones leads downhill at the end of the road.

> **Tip**
>
> Guided groups usually start the route between 10am and 11am and finish around 3pm. You should avoid this period, particularly in high season.

It changes almost imperceptibly into the wide levada path along the Levada do Risco. Here, a narrow path **4** comes up from the left to join yours in a tight bend. However, this route continues further along the levada and into the valley. A couple of minutes later, it comes to a fork **5** where the path to the left heads down to the Levada das 25 Fontes.

In the valley of the Risco waterfall

First of all, however, it's worth taking the **detour to the Risco water-fall**: to do so, follow the levada straight on. Various small streams are channelled into it and dominant vegetation is composed of large tree heath bushes and isolated laurel trees. A right hand bend after solid wood railings provides a first glimpse of the Risco waterfall. Shortly before the waterfall, the wide path swings down to the left **6**. However, your route continues along the levada, but now along its wall (wide and well secured). The detour ends at an **observation platform 7** in front of the waterfall.

Then return via the same route to the fork **5** and the path down to the Levada das 25 Fontes. Follow the sign for 'PR 6 25 Fontes, 2.1 km'. A cobbled path with steps, which may be slippery when wet, then leads downhill.

After a tough but brief descent, you reach the **Levada das 25 Fontes 8**. A wooden sign ('25 Fontes, 1.9 km') points to the right; follow the levada against the direction of water flow. The levada again leads you a level lower into the valley of the Risco waterfall. It crosses the valley by flowing through a pipe; steps lead walkers up to a bridge crossing the river.

Then, on the other side, walk back down to the levada **9**. The levada wall runs between knee and waist height in this section, and serves as a railing as the path narrows significantly. Particularly exposed sections are further secured with solid wire cables.

After a longer, shaded section, the ceiling of vegetation opens up before the levada bends sharply to the right **10** – a narrow path branches off and down to the left, but you continue further along the ▶

Length/walking time: out and back to 3 approx. 8.4 km in 3:00 hrs, or back to 1 in approx. 10.3 km in 3:30 hrs.

Terrain: the walk to the Risco waterfall runs on wide, easy levada paths. The natural stone steps leading down to the Levada das 25 Fontes are slippery when wet. The levada path is narrow and exposed in places but is well protected with wire cable railings.

Marking: none, occasional signs on the route show the way. The walk to the 25 springs is officially called PR 6; the detour to the Risco waterfall is PR 6.1.

Supplies: take everything – no snack bars; the water from the 25 springs is drinkable. WC at 13; you can also walk straight down the steps at 3, turn left at the first house and then take a right.

Getting there: the starting point can only be reached by car. To the Paúl da Serra via Ribeira Brava and the Encumeada pass or via Canhas (signposted) or via Calheta (signposted). On the ER 110 between the Encumeada pass and Porto Moniz, there is a large car park by the turnoff to Rabaçal (opposite a large water basin). The narrow access road down to the houses is blocked off. Taxi rank in Porto Moniz ✆ 291-572540, in Calheta ✆ 291-822129.

The municipality of Calheta operates a shuttle service from the car park to the houses of Rabaçal (return €5, single €3) from 9am to 7.30am, no fixed schedule. The minibus (8 seater) runs continuously in both directions when demand is high. This allows you to skip the walk up from Rabaçal to the car park.

Walk 25

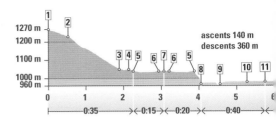

▶ levada to the 25 springs. After a few narrow sections leading up and down, the path comes to a levada bridge. Just at the start, a few steps to the right takes you to the basin of the **25 springs 11**. In fact, there is actually only one single spring source that spurts out in various fountains.

Variants

∗ **Variant:** only the Risco water-fall, out from car park and back in 1:30 hr.

∗∗ **Variant:** only the 25 springs, out from car park and back in 3 hrs.

Then return via the same route to the fork **8** with the path that led down from the Risco levada, where a sign ('ER 110, 3.2 km') points upwards. (If you prefer, climb here and continue back to the start up the path you travelled earlier 1.)

For variety's sake, now take a faster route that climbs up steep **steps** to the houses of Rabaçal; for this ▶

By the Levada das 25 Fontes between waypoints 9 and 10

route, follow the Levada das 25 Fontes. A few minutes later, a cobbled path joins yours from the right at a sharp angle. (It leads up from the Levada Rocha Vermelha, the one below yours.) However, you continue along the same levada and at the same altitude.

The water channel then leads through a narrow wind gap in the rock. Scarcely 5 minutes later, **steps** **12** made of red tuff rock (→ p. 11/12) appear to the left, and the short but steep climb to the houses of Rabaçal begins. (It doesn't matter too much if you walk past these steps – there is a high tunnel entrance about two minutes later, which the levada flows into, and you have to turn round anyway.)

The steps climb through a few winding bends. After a short, intense climb, you soon reach the **Levada do Risco**. Cross the levada using a stepping stone and climb further steps upwards – these are steeper with wire cable railings.

You then reach the yard **13** in front of the WC cabin in **Rabaçal** a few minutes later. Further steps lead up to a house above with an idyllic courtyard. Bear left at the corner of the house and then turn right, heading up wide natural stone steps to reach the access road **3** once again.

You can either wait for the shuttle bus or take the 30 minute walk up the road to the car park **1**. ■

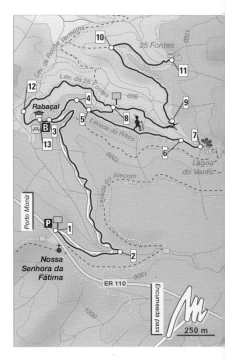

* From the plateau up the Pico Ruivo do Paúl da Serra

This route, though short and easy, still includes all key aspects of a typical Madeira walk: a levada, sun, shade, a summit ascent and views of the central mountain ridge with the island's highest peaks. It's also ideal for children.

► ► The starting point is the stony car park at the **turnoff to the country lodge known as Estanquinhos** ('Posto Florestal Estanquinhos'). A small levada **1** begins directly at the car park, and a narrow dirt path runs beside it. The walk starts off almost flat against the direction of the water flow. After a few steps, a wide path to your right leads away from the levada, though you continue further along the six-inch wide levada for the time being. Up to the right, the Pico Ruivo do Paúl da Serra and its tall pinnacle can already be seen.

The next path to cross yours has nothing to do with your route, which continues along the narrow levada. After a total of 10 minutes, it passes a small birch grove – a rarity on Madeira.

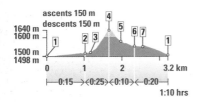

The levada then leads through mixed woodland with numerous pine trees. A **picnic area** ('Área de Lazer Fontes Ruivos') with tables, benches and barbecue towers follows shortly after; locals enjoy grilling Espetada (meat skewers) here on Sundays. Directly after this, a wide dirt track **2** crosses yours.

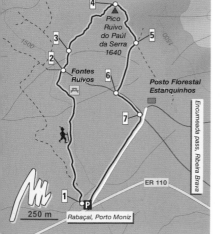

Signs point right towards the Estanquinhos lodge ('Estanquinhos, E. R. 208, 0.5 km) and straight on to this route's destination, the 'Pico Ruivo P. da Serra, 0.7 km' and then on to the Estanquinhos lodge (a distance of 1.6 km over the peak). In any case, the right choice is to continue straight on along the levada. After the picnic area, an oblong-shaped earth reservoir comes into view below, which is not always filled with water. Beyond that, the path crosses a small stream, the 'source' of the levada that begins here **3**.

The route climbs across a shadowless hillside covered in ferns. Even when the summit is within reach, the climb sometimes feels endless – but can be completed in 20 minutes. At the summit of the **Pico Ruivo do Paúl da Serra 4** are boards explaining all the views: to the Paúl da Serra plateau to the north-west, down to

Sporadic clouds over
the north face

São Vicente to the north-east and across to the island's highest peaks to the south-east, though the board says São Vicente again.

Before this viewpoint to the south-east (on the right-hand side as you climbed) is a sign pointing down to the right 'P. F. Estanquinhos, 0.9 km', which you follow. Various trodden paths lead downhill: it doesn't matter which you choose as they all end at a signposted fork **5** in the path.

The route back to the car park bears right at the fork ('Estanquinhos E. R. 208, 0.4 km'): a slight left turn would lead directly to the country lodge.

Having turned right here, the path reaches a wide dirt track **6** about 5 minutes later. Signs here point back to the Fontes Ruivos picnic area to the right. However, the shortest route back to the car park is via the track to the left (signposted as 'Estanquinhos E. R. 208, 0.1 km').

In about 5 minutes you reach the access road **7**. This leads back to the starting point **1** on the right some 10 minutes later. ■

Length/walking time: approx. 3.2 km, 1:10 hr.

Terrain: this route is short and easy; despite this, don't underestimate the climb and descent of the Pico Ruivo do Paúl da Serra, particularly as there is no shade. Orientation is easy in good conditions; you can survey almost the entire walk from here. However, in dense fog – which is not unusual on the plateau – it's possible to get lost, even on this simple route, and there's obviously very little point climbing a panoramic mountain in zero visibility.

Marking: none, occasional signs show the way.

Equipment: sturdy walking shoes, sun protection, esp. for children.

Supplies: take everything, no snack bars.

Getting there: by car from the Encumeada pass, take the ER 101 towards Porto Moniz, past the Bica da Cana viewpoint (signposted). The road's next turnoff is the short road to the Posto Florestal Estanquinhos (this sign cannot be read when heading from the Encumeada pass). Directly by the turnoff is a small, stony car park. No bus connection.

Walk 26

* From Boa Morte to the Cabo Girão

A classic yet easy levada walk along the Levada do Norte via Quinta Grande to the Cabo Girão, the 'Cape of Conversion'. This is not only the island's highest sheer cliff, but is also one of the world's tallest vertical cliffs.

▶▶ From the terminal **1** of bus route 127 in **Boa Morte**, walk up the street a short distance towards São Paulo (signposted). After 5 minutes, the street bends sharply to the left. Below to the right are two large water containers and, a few metres further, the **Snackbar Pinheiro 2** is on the right-hand side of the street opposite a waterworks.

> **Timing tip**
>
> It is best to arrive at Cabo Girão 17 late in the afternoon: the sun's position then provides a better view towards Funchal and, by that time, most of the large tour buses have already left.

A few metres above the snackbar, a concrete road branches off the street to the right and, climbing gently, leads to a fenced-off levada warden's hut. Walk past it to the right; beyond it, the road comes to the wide **Levada do Norte 3**. The route then leads along the levada for some time, following the direction of water flow. If no water is flowing – perhaps on account of maintenance work – walk eastwards.

Terraced fields by the Levada do Norte

After about 20 minutes along the levada, your route crosses a street **4** and continues along the levada on the other side.

After the street, the levada flows through a small side valley and passes by a large water basin (on the right-hand side). At a second levada warden's house, the concrete road **5** is crossed once again. The levada then leads into the wide **valley of Campanário**. On the opposite hillside, the level course of the levada can be seen between the field terraces.

Further into the valley, the levada crosses a dirt path **6** before it enters the main channel of the valley after another bend. The path crosses a road and an overflow channel at a drainage tunnel in the valley floor **7**. (There are also seats here, but a much pleasanter spot for a break can be found at 9).

About 5 minutes later, you come to the first **exposed section**, where the slope to the right drops vertically with no vegetation. However, this passage **8** is only 10–15 m long and should be reasonably easy to cross, even if the railings don't particularly inspire confidence.

Some 15 minutes later, an old cobbled path **9** crosses your route. From here, there is a lovely view of Campanário and also the spectacularly designed motorway. Just afterwards, there is a second **exposed passage**. Railings at knee height at least offer visual reassurance. The tricky sections directly after are very short. After that, you continue on a pleasantly wide path out of the valley.

At a subsequent levada cleaning station, cross another narrow road and immediately come to another, very steep one **10**.

A little later, the levada bends into a second wide valley – the **valley of Quinta Grande**. Ahead and to the right, on the opposite side of the valley, a mountain can be seen with red and white radio masts. Down and to the right of these masts is the viewpoint at the Cabo Girão (not visible from here).

A little further on, your route crosses another old cobbled path **11**; lined with street lights, it is still used as a main connection route.

In the rear valley of Quinta Grande, you come to the old regional road between Funchal and Ribeira Brava. At this point is a bus stop for the Rodoeste bus company.

The levada appears to have disappeared but, if you follow the road down to the left for around 80 m, concrete steps **12** at the vertex of a right-hand bend lead back down to the levada to the right.

A little further on, the levada is covered with concrete girders, meaning that you can walk directly above the channel. ▶

Length/walking time: approx. 12.1 km, 3.20 hrs.

Terrain: this one-way route does not change altitude along the levada, and only a brief climb to the Cabo Girão must be crossed. A head for heights is required in two short sections; a short tunnel must also be traversed.

Marking: none, but the path is clear for the most part.

Equipment: sturdy walking shoes are an advantage. Pocket torch for the tunnel.

Supplies: take water. Snackbar Pinheiro [2] at the start in Boa Morte, open daily in the daytime, ✆ 291-952647; Café/Bar at the Cabo Girão [15], Restaurant Miradouro Cruz da Caldeira with a magnificent terrace opposite the bus stop before [17], open daily in the daytime, ✆ 291-943349.

Getting there: arriving by car via the old coast road between Ribeira Brava and Campanário, signs follow to São Paulo and São João; drive past the sign for Boa Morte up to the Snackbar Pinheiro (opposite the waterworks, down from two large water containers). There are a small number of parking spaces by the bar, otherwise park along the street. However, if you park here, you might find it difficult to return to your car at the end of the walk – therefore, it's better to park in Ribeira Brava (multi-storey car park by the sea, drive towards 'Zona Balnear') and continue by bus (→ p. 29). There is a taxi rank just at the start of the access road to the viewpoint.

Walk 27

▶ A footpath lined with streetlights branches off to the right – don't turn off here, and instead continue along the level of the levada, even when it appears to run through the private land of two houses.

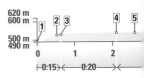

After the second house, the levada is open once again and runs along small field terraces until it reaches a tunnel **13**. It is short, and you can see the other side; however, the ground is so uneven that a pocket torch comes in handy, and helps to traverse the tunnel in a rather long time of 5 minutes. Beyond this, a wide vista opens over the western part of Funchal's hotel district and Câmara do Lobos.

The wide Levada do Norte continues to the left, but at this point leave the levada and bear right, following a narrow side levada. The path is narrow to begin with and, though the slope to the left falls away sharply, it features plenty of vegetation that generally prevents any feelings of dizziness. A little later, scale some concrete steps and follow the wall of the narrow levada onwards. This path is called the 'Vereda Levada do Facho'.

Levada do Norte

The Levada do Norte is one of the island's largest and longest levadas. At the Encumeada pass, it passes from the north side through the mountain and then irrigates fields through to Funchal. When full, some 1,000 litres flows through the levada every second.

A sign for 'Travessa da Levada do Facho' on the corner of a wall points down to the left. The level path then continues straight on for some 50 m up to concrete steps leading up to the right and ending at a road **14**, where you continue to climb up to the right. It leads through the extensive Holiday Property Bond village, composed of numerous three-storey, box-shaped houses with tennis courts and a pool.

After a steep section, it opens up into a road leading to the ER 229. For the detour to the viewpoint at the **Cabo Girão**, walk to the other end of the car park and head through a large iron-barred gate to reach the new complex (entry still free-of-charge at time of research). A souvenir shop, café and toilets await in futuristic-looking buildings. The path takes visitors directly to the **spectacular viewpoint 15**. You can walk out over the 580 m high cliff edge on reinforced safety glass.

Variants

The route crosses numerous streets where walkers can leave the levada and travel back by bus or taxi.

To reach the bus stop on the old road (ER 229) between Funchal and Ribeira Brava, walk back to the car park and then head slightly uphill. The road runs to the left above the hotel area.

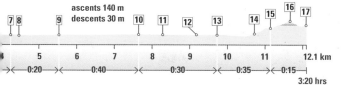

This route's highest point **16** follows after a left-hand bend, and the road descends gently thereafter.

On the road between Funchal and Ribeira Brava, signs point to Câmara de Lobos to the right, while to the left the road heads to Quinta Grande. There is a taxi rank directly beside the T-junction. Bearing right, you pass the turn-off to Fontainhas and Jardim da Serra (signposted) a few metres later. Opposite the turn-off to the ER 229 is Bar Miradouro Cruz da Caldeira and its restaurant. A few steps further down this road towards Câmara de Lobos, the bus stop **17** for journeys back to Ribeira Brava can be found on the left-hand side, and can be recognised by its bench with a roof. ■

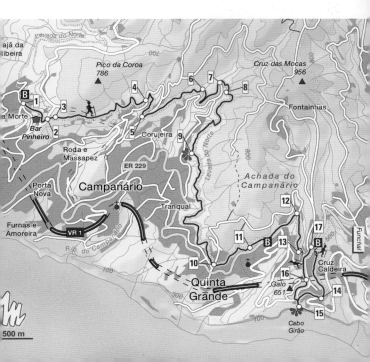

** Circular walk from Fontes

A walk through the mountains far above the Ribeira Brava valley on wide paths with lovely views. It also reaches the summit of the Chão dos Terreiros relatively easily. However, if you don't like cows, you should give the detour to the summit a wide berth!

▶▶ The route's starting point is the centre of the small village of **Fontes** with **Bar Fontes 1**. To the right of the bar, a street leads down into a flat side valley and then up a steeper street, where your route begins. This incline leads past several modern houses, with more traditional buildings sandwiched in between them. The houses and stables thatched with straw are also covered by corrugated iron sheeting. Though this may not appear idyllic, it does mean that the roof lasts longer.

After about 10 minutes, at the last houses in the village, the path flattens out and its asphalt surface ends. The climb then continues up a stony dirt track that has been heavily washed out. Numerous field terraces can be seen on the slope opposite to the left; some lie fallow, though others are still farmed.

It seems as if time has somehow come to a standstill here, as men and women carry heavy loads on their shoulders or heads – though there are also farmers who drive to their fields in a pickup truck.

After 15 minutes' walk, another track **2** joins yours from the right at a sharp angle, but you continue straight on. A further path **3** that joins at a sharp angle from the left is also ignored.

Easy climb up sunny slopes

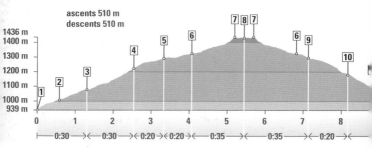

As the route continues, a series of narrow tracks, some overgrown, branch off from yours, but you continue on the main track at all times.

In a sharp right-hand bend **4** there are more views into the valley of Ribeira Brava, the valley of Serra de Água far below and of the Encumeada pass. As the path continues to climb, the view of the pass becomes clearer.

Another sharp right-hand bend follows and offers more lovely views of the same scenery. However, this changes at the third sharp right-hand bend **5**. Ahead is the Pico Grande massif, beyond which the crags of the Pico das Torres (→ Walk 17) lie to the right.

This scenic bend is followed by a level section that even descends for a short time to a small saddle. From here, in a slight bend to the left, you can see the pinnacle of the Chão dos Terreiros along with the highest peaks and the Pico Grande massif to its left.

The path climbs gently once again from this saddle until it reaches a fork **6**, where you turn left, and up to the summit of the Chão dos Terreiros. After almost 80 m, go through a cattle gate. The wide path winds slowly uphill through the pasture land and up to a second cattle gate, which may be hard to open – if so, a makeshift stile made from tree heath helps you over the fence relatively easily.

The path is more heavily overgrown from here on, but remains easily walkable and rises gently until it peters out at a saddle. From here, a trodden path leads up the right-hand crest. However, the pinnacle of the **Chão dos Terreiros** only comes into view towards the very end of the climb, and hides ▶

Length/walking time: approx. 11 km, 3:50 hrs.

Terrain: this circular route leads through gentle, low-mountain landscape on wide paths and forest tracks. The climb features almost no shade. The Chão dos Terreiros is a pasture area. Several cattle gates must be negotiated; some are quite tricky to open, and in such cases stiles usually lead over the fence.

Marking: none.

Equipment: sturdy walking shoes; water, sun and rain protection, perhaps warm clothing due to the altitude.

Supplies: take water; only opportunity to stop for a bite is at Bar Fontes **1** with a small adjacent supermarket at the start and finish; outdoor tables and seating in good weather, (open daily, the staff only speak Portuguese). The bar is the social heart of Fontes!

Getting there: by car via old regional road ER 229 Ribeira Brava – Campanário. The turnoff to Fontes is signposted for São Paulo, São João and Moreno. In the centre of São Paulo, a street branches off towards Espigão/Miradouro Espigão. To reach Fontes, carry straight on and up to a turning area. This is the centre of Fontes (marked with a sign) with Bar Fontes, the starting point of this route. If in doubt about turnoffs, always head uphill! The stretch from the regional road to Fontes is about 8.5 km. There are no practicable bus connections for walkers.

Walk 28

12   1

10   11.0 km

➤← 0:15 ─┤

3:50 hrs

▶ behind a fence . The views from here are also highly impressive. From the summit, an additional five minute detour to prominent crags with extensive views of Madeira's mountain region is worth the effort: follow the trodden path over the mountain ridge. Cross another fence via a stile, after which the path leads slightly downhill. The rocks then lie ahead **8**, and offer a more pleasant spot for a breather than the summit itself.

Then return via the same route through the two cattle gates and down to the main track. The descent is made quickly. Make a sharp left turn on reaching the fork **6**.

After about 100 m, pass through yet another gate. Ignore the track **9** that joins from the right in a sharp angle shortly after. A couple of minutes later, there is another gate by a chestnut plantation.

While the vegetation is rather sparse at higher altitudes, eucalyptus woodland begins after descending 100 to 200 metres. Pass through another cattle gate.

Some 150 m beyond the gate, the track to the **Posto Florestal Trompica** lodge **10** is on the right. A few metres after the driveway to the forest house, a narrow path (leading to Boca da Corrida, the starting point of Walk 21) branches off to the left through broom bushes. However, the tour described here continues along the wide concrete track, where eucalyptus trees are frequently joined by chestnut trees.

At a T-junction **11** with a track from the left, the large tanks of the Reservatório de Água Potável Achada do Boieiro (**drinking water reservoir**) can be seen up ahead. Your route continues directly past the tanks and then heads down the access road leading to them. Ignore tracks branching off from yours.

Madeira's mountain world lies within reach

Soon, the first houses of **Fontes** come into view below. As it continues, the access road comes to a side road **12** crossing it; bear right and follow this road as it undulates through two small side valleys directly back to the starting point **1**. ■

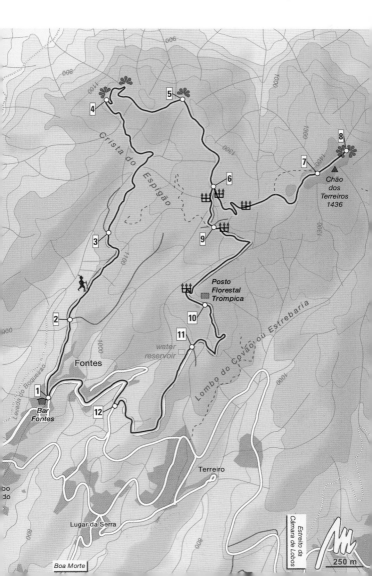

*** From Ponta do Sol to Ribeira Brava

A varied walk through farmland: from the promenade in Ponta do Sol, it curves upwards to the Levada Nova and, after a considerable stretch along the levada, returns back down to the coast.

▶▶ The starting point is the viewing platform **1** over the sea on the coast road in **Ponta do Sol**. Opposite this, an entire row of houses is taken up by the Hotel Baía do Sol. To its left, steps lead to a **church**; walk clockwise around it, then follow the gently-inclined cobbled village street upwards and cross the Ribeira da Ponta do Sol over a bridge.

After the **Centro Cultural John dos Passos**, bear right at the library onto Rua da Marquesa. About one minute later, the river is crossed by

São João – this stream's patron saint

a footbridge leading to a attractively planted car park. On the other side, steps lead up to the old access road to Ponta do Sol.

Bear left on this road **2** and head upwards, then turn right past the car park and lift of the Hotel Quinta da Rochinha (Estalagem da Ponta do Sol). About 20 m beyond the car park by the hotel's steep access ramp, there is an old cobbled path **3** (the first few metres are concrete).

Leave the street here, bearing right and climbing the old cobbled path with the access ramp behind us. It climbs sharply up to the old regional road between Ponta do Sol and Ribeira Brava.

Cross the ER 222 **4**; on the other side, the cobbled path continues as the Caminho de Sto. Amaro and eventually ends at a cul-de-sac in the district of **Lombada** (Caminho do Pico do Melro), which you climb steeply to the left past houses with well-maintained gardens. As the gradient lessens somewhat, there are the first views up ahead of the Quinta do Esmeraldo – a striking building in the classic dusky pink colour of rural Madeiran houses.

The street then descends for a short time. The access road to the Quinta do Esmeraldo then joins from the right; continue straight on. Just before the street bends to the right, a steep, narrow road **5** branches off slightly to the left; you leave the street here and climb further up this road as the gradient steepens once again.

Fork off to the left at a cul-de-sac. Then, before this cul-de-sac leads down to the left, a narrow concrete footpath branches off – you follow it straight on. This path is lined by street lights and bends up to the right up some steps soon after, and is accompanied by a steep, narrow levada.

The path passes a quaint water basin under overhanging rocks and – when almost at the top – bends to the right and comes directly to the **Quinta do Esmeraldo** along a steep, concrete road **6**.

Here, again ascend to the left (a small watermill can be visited behind the house here) and soon come to wide steps leading up to the gate of the **Capela do Esmeraldo**.

Take the street between the Quinta and the chapel, and follow it straight on past a concrete road until a narrow, inclined tarmac street branches off to the left. Follow this street upwards. A footpath with metal railings **7** lined with street lights branches off on a right-hand bend. Here, your route meets Walk 30 (→ p. 156); you can also follow its directions to the Levada Nova.

For this route, however, follow the street another 100 m or so to a fork and then take a few steps to the left. Opposite a recess with a bench and recycling containers, and partly hidden by a house with a flat roof, is the **entrance to the Levada Nova 8**, which you follow out of the valley in the direction of the water flow. Sugar cane is farmed in the surrounding fields.

At a wall, steps lead down from the levada to a narrow cul-de-sac **9**. Turn right here and then turn left at the next village road. After a few steps, the levada accompanies it (to the left) and crosses ▶

Length/walking time: approx. 13.3 km, 4:35 hrs.

Terrain: one-way route with strenuous ascent through Ponta do Sol and Lombada da Ponta do Sol up to the Levada Nova. Narrow levada path with some brief vertiginous sections which require a **head for heights**. Descent to Ribeira Brava on streets and steep paths in places.

Marking: none, occasional signs show the way.

Equipment: sturdy walking shoes, sun and rain protection, poss. poles as your knees will feel the descent!

Supplies: take water; café/bar of the Hotel Baía do Sol **1**, ☎ 291-970140, www.enotel.com; small Bar Café Sítio da Ribeira **14**; numerous cafés, bars and restaurants at the end in Ribeira Brava.

Getting there: by car to Ponta do Sol. There are parking bays on the coast road and a large car park up from the church (turn right immediately after the roundabout towards Vila Ponta do Sol). All parking options are subject to charges. Alternatively, you can drive straight up to the Levada Nova (→ **6** Quinta Esmeraldo). Bus → p. 29.

Getting back: taxi from Ribeira Brava to Levada Nova (approx. €12), taxi rank in Ribeira Brava, ☎ 291-952606, in Ponta do Sol, ☎ 291-972110.

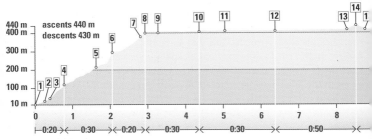

▶ beneath it. Follow the road a little further to a left-hand bend, before which a stairway heads down to the levada to the right (another set of steps after the bend also leads down to the levada).

Following the levada once again, you pass some steps and bend into the deep **valley of the Ribeira da Caixa**. A very short but low tunnel then follows; the path through it is slippery.

At the **head of the valley** 🔟 a waterfall often rains down onto the levada wall. A solid metal bridge cuts this corner so that walkers can negotiate the passage safely.

Moving out of the Ribeira da Caixa valley, the levada path crosses a road **11** that would lead down to Candelária. A short distance later, the levada flows down through a field terrace, which you should avoid:

Small waterfalls often fall onto the path

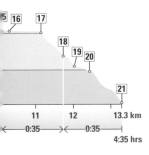

first head up to the left, where a narrow cul-de-sac leads back down to the right.

You then follow the levada round into the deep **valley of Tabua**. In periods of heavy rain, a **waterfall 12** pours out of a steep sided valley – take care in this section.

Just before Sítio da Ribeira, cross a metal bridge over another side valley and you then come to the valley's main arm, which is strengthened with huge concrete walls. Steps branch off to the left before reaching this border and end at a village road which you follow to the right and then cross a bridge over the river. As the road leads onwards, and after crossing the village's tarmac access road, you come back across the levada **13**.

If you would like to stop for a bite, follow the access road uphill (where 'Café' is painted on a wall) to **Sítio da Ribeira**, also called **Ribeira da Tabua**. Walk anti-clockwise around a village church, behind which are steps leading upwards; cross a street and walk further up the steep, narrow cul-de-sac. The **Café Sítio da Ribeira 14** is located on the right-hand side of a flat stretch. It takes a good 5 minutes to reach the café from the church.

Then, after quenching your thirst, head back to the levada **13** via the ▶

Old doorway

▶same route. (Caution! The next section of the path to the tunnel can make some walkers feel dizzy.) After a few short, tight and precipitous passages, the levada is covered with stepping stones and flows about 10 m through a crevice. Further steep passages follow, and then you go through a short tunnel **15**; this takes only a minute or two (pocket torch helpful but not essential).

Beyond the tunnel, a road below runs parallel to the levada. Take care here as the levada wall is narrow. Then cross the road **16** up to the left. A few steps later, steps lead back down to the levada on the other side. Further precipitous passages follow, but these feature solid railings.

After an almost right-angled bend to the left, the path passes fields by the first houses. Walk along a concrete footpath about 1 m lower than the levada; continuing to descend, you come to a set of wide, concrete steps **17**.

The main levada, and with it the level section of the walk, ends here. The steep descent to Ribeira Brava begins to the right, past houses and fields of grape vines and, further down, bananas. Your path then

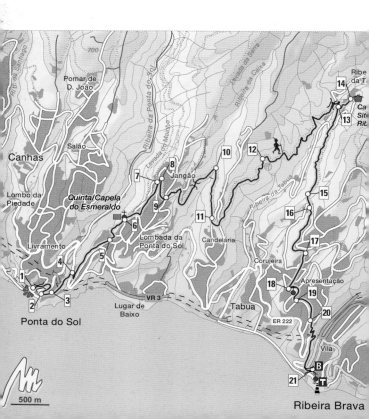

crosses a road several times. As becomes clear further down where there are signposts, this path is the Caminho do Apresentação.

Your route simply continues straight on until the path ends at a street with a relatively new apartment complex made up of uniform buildings **18**. At this point, as you can't go any further (dead end), walk a few steps to the left along the street and then head right down steps to the **church of Apresentação**.

The church of Apresentação

Walk above and to the left of the church, cross the street and, on the other side, walk down the concrete Caminho Manuel Germano footpath.

At the next street **19**, turn left. Some 5 minutes later, in a right-hand curve, the Poço Caminho **20** branches off to the left. Climb up for 40 m (distance, not height) and turn off to the right onto a small street with a dead-end sign. After a few steps, this becomes a steep concrete footpath which provides a first view of Ribeira Brava.

The footpath ends at regional road ER 222, which you walk down to the left until, after about 5 minutes, a cobbled path lined with street lights branches off to the left and allows us to cut off a long bend in the road.

After a few bends, cross a bridge above the **church of Ribeira Brava**. Directly beyond this, above the churchyard, are the bus stops **21**. The taxi rank is situated at the eastern end of the sea promenade. ■

*** A challenging route along the Levada do Moinho and Levada Nova

This levada adventure is best for sure-footed walkers with a head for heights. It leads from the Quinta do Esmeraldo in the valley of the Ribeira da Ponta do Sol river up to the Levada do Moinho and along the Levada Nova back to the starting point. The two levadas feature varied terrain and offer spectacular views.

▶▶ The starting point is the **Capela do Esmeraldo 1** by the Quinta do Esmeraldo in the district of **Lombada da Ponta do Sol**. From the church's courtyard, there is a wonderful view into the deeply cleft valley of the Ribeira da Ponta do Sol river. The **Levada do Moinho** starts behind the church, on the side with the tower, where a small metal gate often stands open. Alternatively, steps to the rear of the Capela lead from the access road up to the levada.

The Levada Nova runs along a sheer rock face

Your route runs along the levada, against the water flow, and into the valley. The path is rather narrow for the first 20 minutes: though protected by railings, watch out for gaps and any sections which may have broken off.

A short damp section then follows in a bend: water always drips down on the levada at this point **2**. In the rainy season, a substantial waterfall also hammers the path here. Shortly after, the view opens to the spectacular route of the Levada Nova. (GPS data may deviate by up to 30 m here!).

The deeper you delve into the valley, the more impressive the scenery becomes. A river **3** is channelled into the levada in a side valley. The overflow must be crossed over concrete stepping stones, after which the levada flows under a scree field for a short time, though the path remains clear.

The river to the left comes gradually closer. After just over an hour and a quarter, the path leads through a striking side valley and, about 5 minutes later, passes an overflow. Take care beyond this point: the climb to the Levada Nova is marked by a stepping stone **4** over the levada. Steep steps ▶

Length/walking time: approx. 7.5 km, 3:00 hrs.

Terrain: circular route. **Surefootedness** is required on the Levada do Moinho, as is a **head for heights** along the Levada Nova . Particularly exposed sections feature wire cable railings.

Marking: none.

Equipment: sturdy walking shoes, poles to balance, rain protection, pocket torch. Perhaps an umbrella for sections passing under waterfalls.

Supplies: take everything, no snack bars. There is only a simple bar at the starting point.

Variants: walk one of the levadas out and back.

Getting there: by car, take the old coast road between Ponta do Sol and Tabua; turn off at the sign for 'Lombada' or 'Levada Nova/Levada Moinho'. After a few bends, this street leads to the flat access road to Quinta do Esmeraldo; turn left here. Parking available in front of the former manor house. No direct bus connection. On foot → Route 29 to 6 .

Walk 30

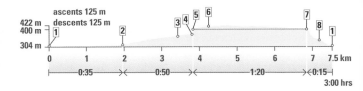

▶ beside this stepping stone lead up to the Levada Nova. (The on-ward path along the Levada Moinho ends after a few metres in any case.) The path then rises steeply, and may be overgrown in places. If it is in good condition, the path soon leads to the **Levada Nova** ⑤ after a series of hairpin bends.

(Here, a **detour to the source of the levada** starts to the left: it passes an equalising and cleaning basin before, a little later, reaching the newly cemented **Madre** (spring). A vast weir spans the river and funnels the water into the Levada Nova. After this detour, return via the same path.) ▶

Levada Nova's most beautiful waterfall, at ⑥

Lombo de São João

900

Ribeira da Ponta do Sol

700

★ Madré

5

4

3

6

Lombo das Terças

700

Levada Nova

700

Pomar de D. João

800

2

Ribeira de Ponta do Sol

600

Levada do Moinho

Levada da Serra

Ribeira da Caixa

7

Jangão

water mill

8

Capela
do Esmeraldo

Lombada da
Ponta do Sol

1

Quinta

amento

ER 222

Candelária

do Sol

100

Ribeira Brava

250 m

Not easy without a bridge – on the Levada Nova

▶ Now walk along the Levada Nova out of the valley; after a few minutes, the levada bends into a wild valley basin where a **waterfall** rains down onto the levada wall **6**. Stepping stones lie across the levada and allow walkers to go behind the waterfall. The path is narrow and may be slippery: **despite the railings, surefootedness and a head for heights are necessary**.

Walk further along the narrow levada wall beneath overhanging rocks and along to a **tunnel**. Though it is straight, and you can see the exit, a pocket torch is useful. You should allow around 5 minutes to traverse the tunnel.

Beyond it, the levada wall becomes the path. Though it is in good condition, several short sections of the stretch up to the first houses in Lombada **require a head for heights**. After the tunnel, the path leads across a solid metal bridge over a side valley. With wonderful views along the way, the path leads to the first houses of Lombada da Ponta do Sol without further difficulty. Here, the levada flows under stepping stones, and five steps lead up to a further steep set of steps crossing your path **7**.

Leave the levada here and head down to the right until you reach a road. The **Capela do Esmeraldo** can be seen straight ahead. Walk further downhill on this road which, after about 5 minutes, bends into a narrow one-way road **8** to the right.

A narrow concrete road (Travessa das Pedras) leads to the access road to the **Quinta do Esmeraldo**. It returns to the starting point **1** shortly after. ■

Safety information

After heavy rainfall, the lower Levada do Moinho may overflow – in that case, you should balance on its narrow wall. This also applies if a section of the path running parallel to it is missing, which is a relatively common occurrence due to the levada's unspoilt nature.

The Levada Nova runs along the vertical rock face for the most part – the levada wall is often the only path. That being said, particularly exposed passages are protected by solid wire cable railings.

✳✳✳ Circular route from Paúl do Mar

This coastal and mountain walk offers a wide variety of sights and features. From Paúl do Mar, the route heads along the seafront to Jardim do Mar, from where it climbs to Prazeres and finally leads back to Paúl do Mar on an old, exceptionally well restored King's Path.

▶▶ The starting point is the boat ramp at the harbour on the south-east edge of **Paúl do Mar**. At the top of the boat ramp, metal steps by a steep ravine lead down to the **beach 1**, which is covered in large stones and rocks. Look along the beach for the best path to the south-east. Walk along and between some large tuff rocks (→ p. 12). Then, after a left-hand bend, Jardim do Mar comes into sight.

Another large tuff rock marks the start of a steep escarpment. The strip of beach becomes very narrow (caution: waves) at the point where the rock face features a near-vertical drop **2**. At **low tide** (→ Box p. 165) **and in calm seas**, this section poses no problems and can be negotiated in less than a minute. However, if you're unsure, it's best to turn back.

The following red tuff rocks, which take rather longer to cross, are best tackled through the middle. At low tide, you can walk directly by the sea – but, if in doubt, scramble over the rocks. Beyond this, the strip of beach widens once again.

As the walk continues, it comes to a so-called alluvial fan **3** – an unmistakeable fan-shaped deposit of sediment below a sheer rock face. Climb to the top of this fan, where there is a trodden path. Then return down to the beach through a thicket of giant cane. The beaten path continues through another, smaller alluvial fan, though you can also continue along the pebble beach. ▶

Length/walking time: approx. 5.8 km, 3:35 hrs.

Terrain: rocky, coarse gravel stretch of coast to Jardim do Mar; climb to Prazeres is steeper, stonier and slippier. The end features a steep descent down a restored King's Path. → Box 'Time window'.

Marking: none. The descent from Prazeres to Paúl do Mar is officially called PR 19.

Supplies: take water; some fishermen's taverns and bars in Paúl do Mar on the access road to the boat ramp; Joe's Bar after 5, open daily exc. Sun, (good!) hot dishes, 12pm–3pm/6–10pm, rustic wooden benches on narrow village path, nice terrace to the rear, e.g. Frango Piri Piri or Lulas (about €8); Bar-Restaurante Vista Prazeres near 10, small covered terrace on the street, simple and quaint; shortly after: terrace bar of the Hotel Jardim Atlântico, ✆ 291-820220, www.jardimatlantico.com, even sweaty walkers are welcome – not quite as rustic but enjoys magnificent views, snacks at reasonable prices, e.g. Prego for €4.

Getting there: take a taxi or drive to Paúl do Mar. Parking by the harbour to the town's south-east or down from the church. Due to the stated time window, it is not possible to travel by bus. Taxi rank in Calheta ✆ 291-822129.

Walk 31

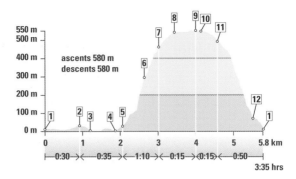

▶ Just before you get to Jardim do Mar, a wide concrete ramp **4** leads up to the promenade, at the very start of which you take the steps to the left up into the village. The Vereda das Pedras branches off, but you should continue straight on. After the Vereda Pôr do Sol, you come to a junction with a fountain **5** bearing the inscription 'CMC 1942'.

If you'd like to stop for a snack, head down to the right here: **Joe's Bar** is just a few steps away. (If you walk past the bar, you soon come to the main square – which appears rather too lifeless for this picturesque village.)

However, if you want to start the climb to Prazeres, head straight on and upwards at the junction with the fountain **5** ('Vereda do Moinho'). A wooden sign points towards Prazeres. A few steps later, a flat path branches off to the right at a crude natural stone wall: at this point, keep left and follow the steps and path uphill. Though meticulously paved in the village, the path's surfacing all but disappears after passing the last houses.

Climb further up steep steps; though a brief flat section follows, steps soon lead further uphill to a viewpoint. The route then crosses a steep slope and heads along a natural stone wall until extremely steep natural stone steps climb once again. Depending on the time of year, this

An idyllic spot: Jardim do Mar

path may be somewhat overgrown, but does ascend rapidly.

After a tough climb, the path leads to a ravine, situated beneath an electricity pylon, with a **tiled mural of Nossa Senhora del Rosário 6**, the patron saint of Jardim do Mar.

The incline lessens a little after this point, though there are several winding bends before you reach a viewpoint **7** below two houses.

From the viewpoint, a footpath with steps leads between the houses to an old cobbled street which leads past more well-tended properties. The surface is tarmacked shortly after and leads to a village street **8** in **Prazeres** that crosses your route.

At this point, bear left as the route finally flattens out. While the traditional natural stone houses to the left of the road are becoming somewhat delapidated, on the right there are new, modern apartment buildings. A little further ahead, ignore a narrow street (Caminho Fundo) branching off from yours where part of the Hotel Jardim Atlântico can be seen to the left. ▶

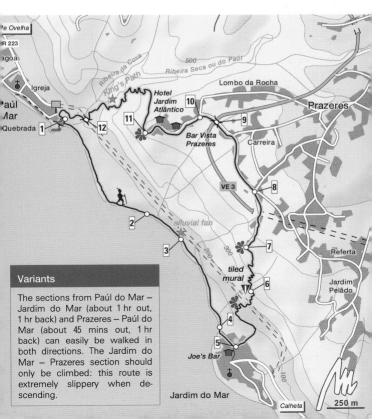

Variants

The sections from Paúl do Mar – Jardim do Mar (about 1 hr out, 1 hr back) and Prazeres – Paúl do Mar (about 45 mins out, 1 hr back) can easily be walked in both directions. The Jardim do Mar – Prazeres section should only be climbed: this route is extremely slippery when descending.

Paúl do Mar harbour

▶ A road bridge **9** leads over the new express road, and a junction **10** follows soon after. Here, bear left and head downhill (Caminho Lombo da Rocha) where, a few steps later, the **Bar Vista Prazeres** is situated to the left.

Continue down this street which, barely 5 minutes later, reaches the car park at the entrance to the **Hotel Jardim Atlântico**, where the lovely, large terrace invites walkers to rest their legs.

At the end of the car park, a board provides information on the ongoing walk down the 'Caminho Real do Paúl do Mar'. A wooden sign beside it guides you to the left and down a road through the hotel's premises. Before bending to the left, this road gives sweeping views into the steep valley of the Ribeira da Cova river: the seemingly inaccessible steep slopes are lined with terraced fields that now lie fallow.

Just before the left-hand bend, turn down steps to the right that lead between the hotel's apartment buildings. Leave the hotel's land at a rubbish bin, and the old, cobbled King's Path then begins.

Right at the **beginning of the King's Path**, there is a beautiful viewpoint **11** to the left with views of Paúl do Mar. The island's authorities have had the path carefully restored in the traditional manner. Its numerous bends and curves lead impressively down the sheer slope, where wire cable railings protect precipitous passages.

After the path has wound back and forth, it's worth looking back into

the steep valley at a point where the tuff is eroded into a bizarre shape. Further down, the path leads over a bridge **12**. On the other side is a levada cut into the tuff rock. Then negotiate a few more steps to reach the **end of the King's Path,** where a board provides information on the route just completed. Turn left at the next junction, and head down the steps to reach the starting point **1** of this walk. ∎

Paúl do Mar to Jardim do Mar – time window

The section from Paúl do Mar to Jardim do Mar can only be walked at low tide and in calm seas. There is a three-hour time window (1:30 hrs either side of low tide). Tide times shift forwards 1 hour over the course of 24 hours. The current tide times are given in local papers 'Diário de Notícias da Madeira' and 'Jornal da Madeira' (generally available for free; low tide = Baixa-mar, high tide = Preia-mar) – or simply ask for information at your hotel. Tide times for Madeira are also given in the windfinder.com weather app. You can find them on various sites online, including www.tide-forecast.com or www.windfinder.com.

Be aware: an ebb tide denotes receding water and retreats over 6 hours; a flood tide denotes rising water and also lasts 6 hours. Low and high tide are precise times which are calculated to the minute, and these are the only times that matter for your route. It's better to start the route in Paúl do Mar and not in Prazeres, as the swell is hard to estimate from up above – even a very rough sea looks as calm as a millpond up at 500 m.

* An easy walk to the island's far west

This is an easy walk along the Levada Nova from Prazeres out to the western-most part of the island at Ponta do Pargo and on to 'A Carreta', a popular restaurant. It's described in three separate stages that are good walks in their own right.

▶▶ **Stage 1: from Prazeres to Lombo dos Marinheiros**: The starting point is by a waterworks, Estação de Tratamento de Águas dos Prazeres **1**. To the right of the waterworks site are steps leading up to the levada – but this path has not always been walkable in the past. You may therefore need to walk back eastwards along regional road ER 101 (also the ER 222) for a stretch and past the turnoff to the Via Expresso. After a few minutes, a second road branches off to the left (Estrada das Eiras/ER 210) towards the plateau, with signposts for Paúl da Serra, Fonte do Bispo and Levada.

> **The three stages**
>
> **Stage 1:** from Prazeres to Lombo dos Marinheiros [14]. Varied section, relatively popular route.
> **Stage 2:** from Lombo dos Marinheiros [14] to Ponta do Pargo [23]. Less frequently walked, through wide valleys.
> **Stage 3:** from Ponta do Pargo to the popular A Carreta restaurant [33]. Usual route due to popular venue at the end; lovely rural scenery. Short enough to walk there and back.

Follow the road uphill for some 100 m; the **Posto Florestal**, the Prazeres forester's lodge, is located on the left. The levada (wooden sign on a lamppost) flows above the lodge **2**; bear left to follow it west in the direction of the water flow. After a few steps, it leads past a levada warden's house; just afterwards, the waterworks you started from can be seen below to the left.

Continue along the levada on a pleasant dirt path. After about 10 minutes, the levada seems to disappear at the ER 101/222 – follow the road in the same direction, cross over a junction where the Caminho Lombo da Velha branches off and, behind a house, you come across the levada once again **3**.

The levada then flows through a valley with mixed woodland of laurel, chestnut trees and Madeira mahogany trees (→ p. 17). Further into the valley, the path crosses a stream. In the summer months it is usually dried up, but after heavy rainfall it becomes a sizeable river; stepping stones in the spillway help you cross. When you walk out of the

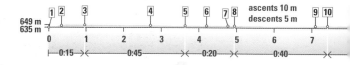

valley, the path passes a levada warden's house that is no longer used. A narrow side street (Caminho Lombo do Coelho do Cá) then approaches from below; you cross it a little later and then continue along the levada, above the regional road.

You cross a steep cul-de-sac near a few houses, and another deep valley then follows. The levada crosses the valley floor as a bridge **4**. Another similar levada bridge follows in the next side valley, though this one is shorter.

Cross a side street on reaching the first houses in the hamlet of **Maloeira**; a sign here points along the levada to Restaurante Solar da Maloeira (✆ 291-872391). The levada is then covered for a short distance, and you cross another cul-de-sac (an arrow points up to the restaurant; if you turn off here, walk about 100m along regional road ER 222 to reach Bar Moinho with a small supermarket.)

The levada then leads into the next deep valley. The vegetation further into the valley is more ancient. The levada spans the valley floor, taking the form of a bridge **5** for the third time on this route.

Walk out of the valley and then, in an immediate right-hand bend, into the next one. After this valley, the path crosses regional road ER 101/222 **6** for the first time, after which the levada flows above a bridge on the new express road (Via Expresso) that then disappears into a tunnel.

The next houses the route comes across belong to the hamlet of Raposeira. The levada is then covered again before reaching a street, which you cross near a school **7**. A few steps later, you have to take a detour at a garden wall as the levada flows straight under the garden: bear left at this wall, walk 30 m up the first side street **8** to the right, and re-join the levada. There is a small ▶

Length/walking time: Stage 1 approx. 12.1 km, 3:10 hrs; Stage 2 approx. 6.5 km, 1:30 hrs; Stage 3 approx. 7.4 km, 2:05 hrs.

Terrain: easy walk with no change in altitude. The entire path is certainly too long to complete in one go, and would become monotonous. It's better to split it into several sections.

Variants: walking the stages separately is recommended.

Marking: none. However, the route is obvious: it follows the levada the whole way.

Supplies: take water; simple Bar Moinho in Maloeira (detour between 4 and 5) and at Lombo dos Marinheiros near 14; simple bars in Ponta do Pargo; the Restaurant A Carreta near 33 is a popular restaurant with a good range of snacks in the adjacent bar, ✆ 291-882163.

Getting there: individually by taxi or car; parking spaces by the waterworks in Prazeres 1, at the picnic area by Lombo dos Marinheiros 14 and in Ponta do Pargo at the start of the last stage 24. Taxi rank Calheta (Estrela), ✆ 291-822129. Bus → p. 29.

Getting back: by taxi, taxi rank Calheta, Estrela district ✆ 291-822129, in Porto Moniz ✆ 291-852243. Bus → p. 29.

Walk 32

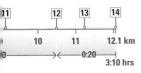

▶ and basic **bar and mini-mercado** on the right a little further up this street.

The terrain along the levada then flattens out and becomes more suited to farming in the small, meticulously constructed field terraces. The path crosses a side street by some farmers' cottages and stables. A valley follows and, at the subsequent mountain ridge, you cross a narrow cul-de-sac near some houses. Take a left-hand bend to re-join the levada. The route crosses another concrete road before reaching the next valley.

After a few side valleys, the levada again forms a bridge **9** to cross a valley floor. This is followed by a narrow valley with a very short stepping stone crossing, beyond which a steep, narrow levada flows to the right. After this valley, cross a wide road **10** leading to Paúl do Mar.

At the following ridge, you pass a levada warden's house with a cleaning station, cross a concrete road and, some 40 paces later, cross another narrow road.

Another valley with two lateral branches then follows: the levada bends sharply to the left in the first arm; two stepping stones make a path across it. At the **Colina da Fajã** country hotel **11**, you leave the levada for a short time and head down to the left. Cross the hotel car park and climb steps back to the levada. A little further on, cross another narrow, steep side street. Two more side valleys follow before you cross a narrow concrete path; after a few more bends the levada leads into the deeply cut valley of the Ribeira

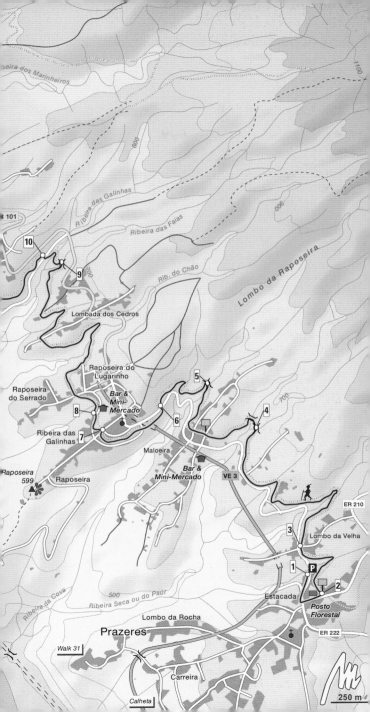

Along the Levada Nova

▶ dos Marinheiros river. Before heading further into the valley, cross the ER 101/222 **12** once again.

The levada forms a bridge **13**, complete with railings, to cross the river again. On the other slope, you meet the regional road again at **Lombo dos Marinheiros 14**, where there is a lovely viewpoint with picnic tables.

Follow the ER 101/222 up a few metres to the right to reach the continuation of the levada on the left. A little further on, there is a bus stop on the left of the street. The simple **Bar Os Marinheiros** lies diagonally across from it. ■

▶▶ **Stage 2: from Lombo dos Marinheiros to Ponta do Pargo**: From the picnic area **14** by the ER 101/222, follow the road upwards a few metres towards Ponta do Pargo to find the entrance to the levada on the left. Cross a concrete footpath a few minutes later. Shortly after, the path leads around a relatively new complex **15** by the name of Vivenda Andrade. A stretch further on, steps lead to a concrete road. On the other side, walk a short distance up an access ramp to a house; steps in front of it lead back to the levada.

Cross another valley down from the regional road. Soon after, the first houses of the hamlet of Amparó can be seen on the mountain ridge opposite. The path then reaches regional road ER 101/222 **16** and continues on the other side.

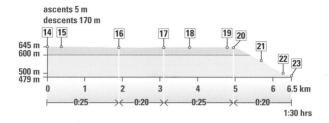

There then follows another deeply carved valley with two vast branches; in the second valley branch, cross a river **17** that sometimes holds a considerable amount of water.

The first house of **Amparó**, the Casinha do Amparó, is almost a small estate with a well-maintained garden. However, many of the old houses have been abandoned.

Later on, the levada runs parallel to a road and comes across a cul-de-sac **18**, which you cross before walking round a wide valley with two side arms.

Beyond this, cross a concrete road **19**. The path later leads through a meadow that is occasionally used as pasture land. After this, the levada runs above a road in the district of **Corujeira de Fora**. At the point where a narrow levada joins from the right, climb down steps to the left that lead down to the road **20** and follow it downhill to the right. In the left-hand bend that follows, a dirt track joins the road from the right and leads back up to the levada. If you'd like to continue on to the A Carreta restaurant and bar, climb a few metres back up to the levada and follow the **directions in Stage 3**.

If, on the other hand, you'd prefer to descend to Ponta do Pargo, walk along the street until you reach the village. Directly after the dirt path at the end of the bend in the road, pass a large water basin and a waterworks (Estação de Tratamento de Água de Ponta do Pargo).

Further down, the road forks: continue straight down at the fork **21** (Rua Salão de Cima), and walk past the wall of the Quinta da Serra. After the wall, the angular church tower of **Ponta do Pargo** comes into view on reaching the village's first houses.

Continue along the road. When you reach a public well with a tap, bear right and head downhill, where the street passes an orange and white transmission mast. Bear left at the fork that follows to return to regional road ER 222/101 **22**. Immediately on the right is a simple little bar, while the **church** is straight ahead.

Follow the right-hand bend past the church and then straight on through the village; at the turnoff to the lighthouse (signposted as 'Farol') is the bus stop **23** for the 16:45 service to Funchal. ∎

▶▶ **Stage 3: from Ponta do Pargo to the A Carreta restaurant**: If you wish to start the last section from Ponta do Pargo, walk or drive up the street that leads from the village church in Ponta do Pargo over regional road ER 222/101. Continue uphill the whole way and past the waterworks (Estação de Tratamento de Água de Ponta do Pargo); just after it (some 1.3 km from the ER 222), a stony dirt road **24** joins from the left in a right-hand bend (parking space here; waypoint **20** of Stage 2 is about 15 m away). This area is called **Corujeira de Fora**. The road leads up quickly to the levada; you follow it north, walking in the direction of water flow. At the start, the levada follows an unusual zig-zag route. After a few minutes, it passes a small, idyllically located, levada warden's house, and a large water basin can be seen below to the left.

After this, the levada flows into the wide **valley of the Ribeira dos Moinhos** river. Numerous field terraces can be seen lying fallow on the opposite side of the valley. The levada again forms a bridge to cross the valley floor of a narrow side valley. A little later, it passes a picturesque levada warden's house **25**, though it is no longer used. Shortly after, there is a series of gates with cattle grids over the levada.

The valley of the Ribeira dos Moinhos river is not inhabited; the scenery is rolling hills with mixed woodland composed of eucalyptus and pine trees. Further into the valley, Madeira mahogany and Canary laurel trees (→ p. 17) also appear. The levada crosses the riverbed as a bridge **26** – it is about 10 m long and has no railings, so **take care**.

In the valley's second side branch, cross a river over its spillway **27**. During the rainy season, this section can be **rather tricky**: look for the best route over the stones. In the third side branch, a **waterfall 28** splashes down onto the levada, though it is often dried up in summer. Some of the slopes the route passes when walking out of the valley are used as pasture land for animals.

After rounding the valley, the surrounding terrain becomes rather flat by Madeiran standards. Here, the levada flows through a very low, short but impassable tunnel, and the path leads around the outside. Just after the tunnel, the path crosses a track **29**, followed shortly after by another road **30**, beyond which is a large, concrete water basin.

The following levada bridge with stepping stones doesn't cross a valley floor, but instead leads over a dirt track. After a few less pronounced ▶

A welcome opportunity to refuel: the A Carreta restaurant

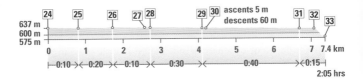

▶ valleys, the path crosses a washed-out road **31**. At the next wide road, leave the levada and bear left. A weathered metal sign **32** points towards the 'Restaurante'.

The road descends sharply and soon reaches the ER 101 **33**. The **A Carreta restaurant** (with a bar and rooms for overnight stays) is just a few steps to the left. The bus stop is diagonally opposite (Timetable → p. 29; according to the barmaid, services to Ponta do Pargo at 13:45, 14:30 and 15:30 – not all services are shown in timetables, and the locals often have insider knowledge). ■

Levada warden's house in the valley of the Ribeira dos Moinhos river

*** Along the Levada da Fajã Rodrigues into the Ribeira do Inferno valley

Short levada tunnel adventure at São Vicente. The Ribeira do Inferno flows through one of the island's last untouched valleys of endemic laurel forest and dense undergrowth.

▶▶ At the end of the street (parking available) by the **Parque Empresarial de São Vicente** is the start of a track **1**, which you climb for

about 10 minutes until it is crossed by the levada; at this point, a board gives information on the route. On the other side of the track is the signposted start **2** of the levada path. Walk along it against the direction of water flow. After a few minutes, a wide water staircase channels water into the levada; this water comes from a tunnel driven 1,700 m into the mountain.

On the Levada da Fajã Rodrigues

Numerous lily-of-the-valley trees (→ p. 14 and photo on p. 18) grow further along the

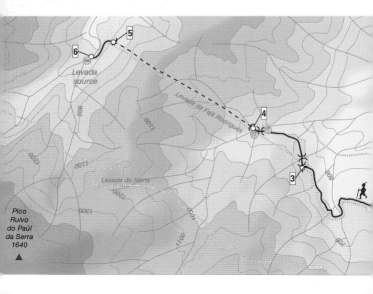

levada. The path then passes a hillside that often suffers from land-slips. At this point, the levada is covered or buried under boulders for a short time.

A steep rock basin then follows, where a **waterfall** rains down onto the levada path. You can pass behind the waterfall, but be careful – the **path is slippery**.

There are several vertiginous passages to get by. Though the railings might be in poor condition if they have not recently been maintained, the path is wide and the levada wall runs at knee- to hip-height, which creates a useful handhold.

You reach the first tunnel **3** soon after. It is barely 50 m long, but the path through it is very narrow. However, as long as you take care not to bump your head or shoulders, it is quickly crossed.

A few paces further, the covered levada flows into the route's second tunnel. It measures some 150 m and, for a longer section in the middle, stepping stones lie across the levada and make walking easier. Sharp stones jut out of the roof: **make sure you mind your head!** This tunnel is also quickly traversed.

Beyond it, the levada is often covered. Several vertiginous passages are made safe, though others are not. The path then ▶

Length/walking time: there and back via same route, approx. 8.2 km, 3:40 hrs.

Terrain: this levada walk isn't particu-larly demanding, but includes some vertiginous passages. Dangerous sections are protected with railings (some are in poor condition). Water-falls cascade onto the path at certain times of year. Three short tunnels and one long one must be traversed. Tall walkers will have to stoop; the path through the tunnels is narrow. Risk of falling rocks in some places. No GPS signal from **4** onwards.

Marking: none. However, the route is clear, always follows the levada. Its official name is PR 16.

Equipment: sturdy walking shoes, sun protection, rain protection even in good weather because waterfalls are passed, pocket torch with spare batteries.

Supplies: take water; bar with Mini-Mercado Miradouro, 700 m before the end of the road **1**, ☎ 291-846527.

Getting there: by car, on old regional road ER 104 take the signposted turnoff towards Ginjas and Lanço. The Centro de Saúde of São Vicente is by the turnoff. After about 800 m, don't turn right to Lanço, instead continue for 2.5 km towards Parque Empresarial. When you get there, park on the side of the street/track at the end of the street. Taxi rank in São Vicente ☎ 291-842238. No direct bus connection.

Walk 33

► leads into a steep side valley densely populated with laurel trees (→ p. 16). Further into the valley is a waterfall and then the third, very short tunnel. At the end of it, a beautiful waterfall pours into an equalising basin. You walk through a wild, picturesque valley along a short bend and then reach the entrance **4** to the long, fourth tunnel.

Water from the humid walls drips continuously onto the path at this point. This straight tunnel is about 1,100 m long, though the other end can already be seen at the entrance. However, you must gear yourself up for **20 minutes of darkness**. Water drips from the roof at some points inside, and some stepping stones lie across the levada and widen the final section of the path.

After the end **5** of the tunnel, the levada is again covered and runs along the steep eastern face above the **Ribeira do Inferno valley**, one of the most primordial valleys on Madeira: dense laurel forest grows over the slopes, various ferns decorate the humid walls – and all in dark green. Ethereal clouds of fog often waft into the valley.

The steep eastern face of the Ribeira do Inferno valley beyond
waypoint 5

You then cross another small side valley. (A brick-built water intake is
a better stop to take a break than the end of the route, where there is
little space.) After this, the levada flows below overhanging rock and
soon reaches the **source of the levada** 6. The river that runs through
a narrow gorge at this point is funnelled into the levada. Follow the
same path back to the start. ■

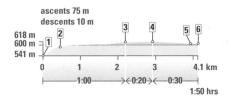

* Along the Levada da Central da Ribeira da Janela

This is an easy levada walk from Lamaceiros above Porto Moniz into an untouched part of the island. The route is straightforward and consequently offers a good opportunity to get to know the vegetation in the laurel forest. It's also ideal for children, who definitely have an advantage in the two tunnels.

▶▶ The starting point is at the sprawling picnic area **1** by the waterworks (and reservoir) of **Lamaceiros**. The start of the walk can be found at the point where the levada crosses the access road in a right-hand bend. A sign that reads 'Antenção Perigo de Queda e Afogamento' warns against falling and drowning. I have never let this discourage me; indeed, I've guided several walking groups along the levada over the years and though some have been up to their waists in water, nobody has drowned on me yet!

> **Tip for children**
>
> The very start of the walk is a great place to look for eucalyptus seeds. Seeds with 3 and 6 apertures are very special: just like four-leafed clovers back home, they are said to bring good luck. Seeds with 7 apertures are even rarer — it took this author 17 years to find one!

Looking back on the levada between waypoints ④ and ⑤

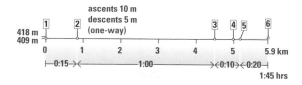

To begin with, the path is wide, lined by hydrangeas, and leads through a eucalyptus forest. The levada's gradient is barely perceptible, and you walk against the water flow. After a few minutes, you pass the first of the picnic tables and a first levada cleaning station then follows, complete with an equalising station and a grid to collect the leaves. A first scenic viewpoint **2** – with views of the village of **Ribeira da Janela** on the opposite slope and into the deep, dark-green valley with the same name – follows shortly after.

The path continues to pass picnic tables and rubbish bins: the laurel forest (→ p. 16), which is well worth protecting, stays fairly clean as a result. The levada is covered for a short passage where earth and stones often fall from above. The further you walk into the Ribeira da Janela valley, the more impressive the primeval landscape becomes. A passage in the vertical rock face then follows, though it is well protected with railings. For the most part, though, the path runs through dense laurel forest.

You reach the first tunnel **3** in a narrow side valley. A rather challenging-looking concrete section leads to the tunnel entrance. The tunnel itself is straight, and the other side can be seen from the start. It takes around 10 minutes to walk through the tunnel; low sections, puddles and uneven surfaces prevent fast progress.

The tunnel ends in a spectacular side valley **4** where a waterfall gushes down onto the levada ▶

Length/walking time: out and return via same route, approx. 11.8 km, 3:30 hrs.

Terrain: easy levada walk with two tunnels. The levada also leads against the vertical rock face for long sections, though the path is made safe and wide up to the first tunnel. Expect puddles in the tunnels. The path narrows after the tunnel but is well protected. A head for heights is an advantage due to plunging views, though there is no real danger. Risk of rockfalls in some places in windy and rainy conditions.

Marking: none, but the route along the levada is clear.

Equipment: sturdy walking shoes, pocket torch (tunnels are tricky without one).

Supplies: take everything; no snack bars along the route. Simple bar by the reservoir at the start **1**.

Getting there: by car or taxi from Porto Moniz, take the ER 101 towards Santa Madalena (actually Santa Madalena, simply signposted as Santa, as everyone refers to the town). The road to Lamaceiros (signposted) branches off at a roundabout. Signs for 'Estação Tratamento de Água' then follow. Large picnic area with parking and WC at the very start of the route. Lots of locals grill meat skewers (espetadas) here on Sundays. Taxi in Porto Moniz, 📞 291-852243. Bus connections unhelpful for walkers.

▶ in the rainy season. A temporary corrugated iron roof protects against extreme drenchings.

The next tunnel **5** is in the same valley and follows immediately after. This one is traversed faster, but does bend, meaning that the other end can't be seen at first.

Even further along the levada

You can continue along the levada past this route's turning point, and walk until you tire or run out of time. More tunnels follow along the levada after waypoint ⑥; some are downright hazardous and wet. It is possible to walk along the levada and climb up to the spring at Fonte do Bispo on the north-west edge of the plateau. However, this path is 25 km long and difficult for individual walkers to organise as an entire route. What's more, you should ask levada workers about the condition of the paths through the route's tunnels before starting this long walk.

After the second tunnel, the path runs in the vertical rock face for a time (protected with railings, **head for heights beneficial**). The path here is narrower.

After a few bends, it comes to a levada warden's house **6**. It is rarely occupied, and is only really used when extensive work to the levada is required. Avocado and annona trees grow on the hillsides. The front yard of the house provides another lovely view

Steep valley head between the first and second tunnels

of the impressive valley. The house is a good place to rest before turning around and heading back to the starting point **1** via the same route. ∎

*** From Achadas da Cruz down to Porto Moniz

This walk crosses the Ribeira do Tristão river valley, a protected conservation area with coastal vegetation, and leads on to Porto Moniz with its popular ocean swimming pool.

▶▶ The starting point is the **summit station** of the two-cabin cable car in **Achadas da Cruz**. An information board shows that the path downhill is, in fact, the Vereda do Calhau. (The stated 4.5 km and 2 hrs include both climb and descent!) Concrete steps lead up to the footpath **1** that starts just to the right of the station. Tuff, dirt and rock steps soon lead downhill in a series of steep, winding bends. After descending for about 30 minutes, it seems as if the path might disappear into the Atlantic. The path runs towards a sheer face for about 2–3 minutes, and is extremely narrow. However, just when you think that it can't continue, the path bends to the right.

More bends then follow. The further you descend, the more dominant the native coastal vegetation becomes, with smooth spear-leaved spurge, globularia and aeoniums (→ p. 15). A path **2** branches off to the right at a sharp left-hand bend. Note this point: the climb to Santa begins here.

Before that, though, treat yourself to a **detour to see the impressive meeting point of the Ribeira do Tristão** river and the sea. The last of the 100 metres to the mouth of the river are down steep stone steps. It's worth walking a short distance into the deeply carved river valley – depending on the water level, there might be a waterfall further in.

A few steps continue the sharp descent to the exceptionally coarse pebble beach **3**. **Caution**: it's too dangerous to bathe here.

A lovely view of Porto Moniz

If you'd like to return to the starting point from the coast with the cable car, → see Variant 1; however, the journey is not for the faint-hearted.

For the climb to Santa, return to the path branching off uphill at **2**. This means leaving the path you followed from Achadas da Cruz and bearing left.

Climb uphill for a few steps, though the route soon levels out and crosses a steep hillside. The slope to the left falls away sharply to the Ribeira do Tristão valley floor. Railings provide protection in places with vertical drops. Then climb once again before walking down into the valley floor **4**.

The climb to Santa begins on the other side of the river. Climb steeply up steps and through bends – followed by more steps and more bends – without shade and head up to a road on a wide rock spur. There are picnic tables just a few steps to the left.

Continue up to the right and pass by a street that ends here until, after about 60 m, you come to concrete steps **5** on the right leading to a narrow levada. Walk along on a narrow, stony dirt path past some field terraces where there are more lovely views of the coast and the path that led down from Achadas da Cruz.

This route allows you to cut off a long bend in the road. It then leads directly to a concrete wall supporting the road before crossing a small levada below the wall. Bear left at this point and continue above the small levada, then turn right, cross another narrow levada to reach the viewpoint of **Santa** at the end of the village street.

Leave the viewpoint and continue along the street. A few paces further, keep right at a fork in the street **6** and walk on a tarmac ▶

Length/walking time: approx. 7.2 km, 3:15 hrs.

Terrain: one-way walk with a slippery decline at the start. The hillsides generally fall away sharply and even vertically in some places; railings in parts. Demanding climb through steep winding bends. From Santa Madalena to Porto Moniz, the route follows roads with little traffic and an old cobbled path (slippery when wet).

Marking: none; occasional signs show the way.

Equipment: sturdy walking shoes, sun protection as some long sections offer no shade.

Supplies: take water; Snackbar Achadas da Cruz Calhau by the summit station **1** of the cable car at the start; simple bars and mini-mercados in Santa Madalena on the path to regional road ER 101 and the ER 101 itself; numerous bars and restaurants in Porto Moniz.

Getting there: by taxi or hotel bus from Porto Moniz to the start, the teleférico in Achadas da Cruz. By car, take the ER 101 to Achadas da Cruz and follow signs for 'Teleférico'. It is a good 2 km from the ER 101 to the starting point. For those arriving by car, there are various ways to shorten the route. Taxi rank in Porto Moniz ☎ 291-852243.

Getting back: either take the cable car from Quebrada Nova back to the start (€3, only early morning or 1pm-8pm) or a taxi from Santa either to the start (about €10–15) or somewhere else.

Walk 35

The surf at the mouth of the Ribeira do Tristão river

▶ surface through Santa. The narrow street leads past strangely insubstantial-looking houses.

Continue past a few streets without turning off. Just after the Caminho do Lombo Brazil, **Bar Costa** with a mini-mercado **7** is located on the left of the road. Then continue along the street, without turning off, until you reach the **church of Santa** by regional road ER 101 **8**.

The **Bar Restaurante Residencial Fernandes** is opposite the church on the ER 101. Should you wish to return to the start at this point, there are usually some taxis here (if you drove to the starting point in a rental car, you should consider whether you want to make the descent to Porto Moniz).

Variant 1 with the cable car

If you'd like to return to the start with the cable car, make a sharp left turn at the beach ③ and head directly along the steep rock face. At the point where the cliff face is intersected by a vast alluvial fan by the name of Quebrada Nova, natural stone steps lead up to a path. The cable car's summit station can be seen to the left. Then, after a left-hand bend, the valley station comes into view. If there's nobody here, you need to make yourself noticeable somehow. There is a radio device in the gondola that you can use to contact the summit station. You need a **good head for heights** for the journey – the gondola doors haven't always shut in the past. If this option sounds too daring for you, walk back via the same route or follow the main route on-wards.

Then bear left on the ER 101 and head down towards Porto Moniz, past the BANIF bank to the next village street branching off (Caminho Irmã do Perpétuo Socorro) **9**. Leave the ER 101 at this point and head left. The village street leads straight downhill and over a crossroads. Metal signs remind you that you're walking down the Caminho do Pico.

After passing the last houses in Santa, the street becomes a concrete road **10**. A few steep bends then lead downhill before the road ends at a viewing platform that provides further views of Porto Moniz. From here, steep steps lead down a cobbled path and end at a street **11** in the upper part of Porto Moniz.

Follow this road down to the left and, shortly before the village street meets the ER 101 main road once again, bear left on a concrete road. It runs just below and parallel to the ER 101, and then meets the Caminho da Pedra Mole **12**, which you follow downhill.

This caminho is a picturesque cobbled path that heads along past the uppermost houses in **Porto Moniz** and directly towards the church. Here, the road surface is tarmacked once ▶

Red tuff rocks in the Ribeira do Tristão ravine

Colourful field terraces

Variant 2 with a taxi

Only walk as far as regional road ER 101 in Santa **8** and take a taxi from there back to the start **1**; see above.

A rather unusual open-air pool: the ocean swimming pool at Porto
Moniz

▶ again; head down to the right, walk past the church and the street
soon reaches the taxi rank by the Banco Espirito Santo.

At this point, don't head right on regional road ER 101; instead, bear
left onto the Rua do Lugar da Bica and walk past the garden wall of an
old ramshackle quinta. The village's health centre (Centro de Saúde)
follows soon after. Just beyond it, bear right at a junction **13** and follow
the Rua de Dr. Cosme downhill.

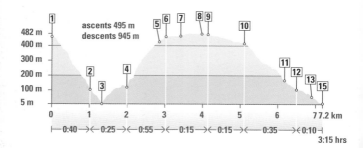

A right-hand bend follows just after; cut the corner by heading down the Beco do Lugar, a narrow concrete path with steps. Lined by street lights, it looks like a private path; it is, however, a public route open to everyone and cuts off a long corner in the street.

It meets the street diagonally across from the Residencial Gaivota with its bar and restaurant in the lower part of **Porto Moniz**. Bear left here and, a few steps later, you'll reach a roundabout, shortly after which is the **ocean swimming pool** **14**. ■

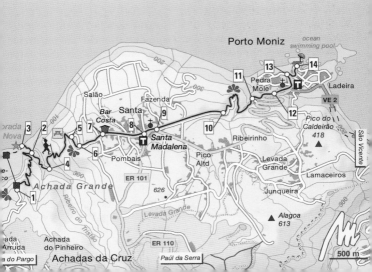

*** On the Caminho do Norte from the Encumeada pass down to São Vicente

This route offers an intense laurel forest experience, descending from the Encumeada pass to São Vicente. Although it is one of Madeira's officially mapped walking routes, relatively few walkers undertake it. Consequently, even the timid Madeira laurel pigeon can be seen on this peaceful hike.

▶▶ When you reach the **Encumeada pass**, turn towards Paúl da Serra and walk that way for a few metres to reach the route's starting point **1**, where a board provides information on the path ahead. Down to the Ribeira Grande, at an altitude of 320 metres, the path is the official PR 21.

Directly beside the board, stone steps lead down the northern face of the pass. To begin with, the steep slopes are covered in tree heath and heather, though laurel trees soon begin to appear. The steps turn into an old cobbled path that leads to a set of dirt steps shortly after. Following this, the idyllic path goes downhill through dense **laurel forest** with typical vegetation (→ Box p. 193). In late summer and

early autumn in particular, Madeira blueberries can be plucked from bushes at head height. Relatively noisy Madeira laurel pigeons regularly flit here and there as they flee from unfamiliar walkers through the forest. If you look carefully, you can see that this track is actually an old cobbled path; it once represented an important connection between the north and south of the island. The tourist authority had it repaired for walkers fairly recently.

Almost 15 minutes later, you cross a forest aisle before some steps lead further down into the forest. Walk over rocky ground down the path, which has been washed out to form a ravine. Barely 10 minutes after the forest aisle, cross a steep side valley **2** where the view to the right opens up to the dark-green slopes of the São Vicente valley basin for the

The path through the laurel forest

first time. Soon after, though, the path delves back into the dark, mystical forest. Turn right immediately after: a low stone wall runs straight across the path that appears to continue straight ahead.

At this point, your route swivels onto a clear path to the right. A few metres further on, due to the steep gradient, the path steps are made of wooden beams – an unmistakeable sign that you're on the right track. A turnoff **3** to the Chão dos Louros picnic area (about 1 km on path PR 22) soon follows. Immediately after, regional road ER 228 (formerly ER 104) from São Vicente to the Encumeada pass comes into view. Steep steps lead down to the road.

Climb a short section up the road **4** to the right ('Ribeira Grande 2.1 km'), and follow it through a left-hand bend to the continuation of the footpath on the left. Then walk through a gate and a few metres along a wide forest track. However, keep left at a fork ('Ribeira Grande 2 km') **5** and walk down into the dense laurel forest once again. The path is very wide in this section, as it is occasionally used by forestry workers. Some specimens of the lily-of-the-valley tree (Clethra arborea) also thrive here; its blooms are reminiscent of the lily-of-the-valley flower and usually appear between July and September. Though the tree is not a species of laurel, it is at home in this vegetation zone.

A few minutes after the fork, pay close attention: the track you walk down makes two consecutive right-hand bends before a concrete bridge leads over a side valley. However, before the side valley with the concrete bridge, steps **6** supported by wooden beams lead down into the forest. A cairn marks the start of the steps – there are no signs or other markings. In any case, you follow the steps downhill. ▶

Length/walking time: approx. 7.6 km, 2:30 hrs.

Terrain: long descent of 1,000 metres in altitude. The path is well maintained, and particularly steep sections feature steps. Despite this, surefootedness is required. From Ribeira Grande 8 on, the route follows village roads with little traffic.

Marking: red-yellow coloured markings and signs up to Ribeira Grande 8.

Equipment: rain and wind protection. A large part of the walk leads through the humid laurel forest; the ground is often wet and slippery, so non-slip, ankle-high walking shoes are advisable. Walking poles are helpful due to the long descent.

Supplies: large souvenir shop at 1 which sells snacks and drinks. Some places to stop for a bite in São Vicente. Directly by the church: Café/Bar Estoril.

Getting there: by car, drive to the Encumeada pass. Just above the pass on the road to the Paúl da Serra (ER 110), there is a pull-off opposite the souvenir shop. From São Vicente back to the start, take bus line 6 at about 15.30 or a taxi (approx. €18). Taxi rank in Ribeira Brava ☏ 291-952349, in São Vicente ☏ 291-842238; Gilberto Andrade is a multilingual (EN, FR, IT, ES) taxi driver in São Vicente (mobile ☏ 963-671604, gilbertoandrade64@hotmail.com). Bus connections to the starting point → p. 29.

Walk 36

Ribeira Grande – in spite of the name, it is only a small village

► The further down you walk, the more conifers grow in the laurel forest; these are Mediterranean beach pines, which are not endemic and have been introduced. Walk past a clearing where the view again opens up to the surrounding slopes.

Shortly after, a narrow side road – gravelled in places – runs below and to the left of the footpath, which soon comes down to meet it.

Bear right on the road (caution: no markings and no signs). After only a few minutes, turn off down steps **7** created for the footpath and made safe with wire cable railings. Below to the right, a stream splashes and gurgles. Steep steps lead downwards, and you cross the stream. To the left of the ford, the stream pours over a ledge and into the valley as a waterfall. Walk further down the steps on the path until you come to the end of another forest track. Continue straight on along a

ascents 5 m
descents 950 m

1008 m
900 m
800 m
700 m
600 m
500 m
400 m
300 m
200 m
100 m
54 m

0   1   2   3   4   5   6   7   7.6 km

├─0:30─┤├─0:25─┤├─0:35─┤├──0:30──┤├──0:30──┤

2:30 hrs

narrow pathway. By this point, the laurel forest has been replaced entirely by eucalyptus trees. However, the path soon bends to the right into a narrow, idyllic valley with typical laurel forest vegetation.

After a subsequent left-hand bend, there is a first view of the houses and, further into the valley, a church tower appears. It belongs to the Fátima chapel of São Vicente.

A steep cobbled path then leads down through tight curves to the first houses in Ribeira Grande. There is a small square here with a public watering place, a table and two benches **8**.

A narrow concrete road leads past a few houses in **Ribeira Grande** to a turning place with a bus stop (unfortunately, departure times are not convenient for walkers). Walk down and out of the valley along the approach road to the village up to a junction **9** with three other roads. Choose the middle road of the three, which leads downhill to the left of the river. Walk past a construction materials company ('blocos' – concrete bricks typically used to build houses quickly and cheaply – can be seen from the road). ▶

The laurel forest – a prehistoric habitat

The laurel forest is the most typical, primordial form of vegetation on Madeira. At one time, such vegetation spread across the entire island above an altitude of about 400 m, and gave the island its name ('Madeira' is Portuguese for wood).

The laurel forest is a relic of the Cenozoic era: during the Ice Ages, such woodland came from Central and Northern Europe, but was able to survive on the Azores, on the Canary Islands as well as on Madeira.

Ecologically, it is situated between mountain forests in the tropics and the evergreen forests of the Mediterranean. The trees in the laurel forest barely show annual rings, and have comparatively thin bark. A further characteristic is the trees' leathery leaves with drip tips. The most common species on this route is the Canary laurel (Laurus novocanariensis), previously known as the Azores laurel. It can grow up to 25 m tall on Madeira, and its fruit is reminiscent of olives.

Its epiphytes – mosses and ferns – are also typical for laurel forests. The most impressive fern species on this route is the European chain fern (also known as the rooting chain fern, Woodwardia radicans). Its fronds can grow up to 3 m in length. Like the laurel forest itself, it is a relic of the Cenozoic era, when it was spread across Central Europe. Today, however, it can only be found in humid valleys on the Canary Islands, the Azores and here on Madeira.

At drier places or locations more exposed to the wind – such as the very start of this route – the laurel forest degenerates and creates the Fayal-Brezal zone, where bog myrtle and heather bushes in particular can thrive.

▶ Beyond it, the road crosses the river; walk downhill to the VE 4 express road **10**.

Head down to the right on the VE 4. The following about 800 m long section is less attractive, as it simply leads along the express road; however, there is little traffic, and walkers can continue undisturbed along the verge. In a good 10 minutes, this section is behind you.

After the 14 kilometre marker, the road comes to a roundabout **11**. The road to the left leads to the Estalagem do Vale; to the right – your route – heads towards 'Grutas de São Vicente'. Just after the roundabout, a narrow road to Lameiros branches off to the right –

you could follow it to make a detour to the Fátima chapel. However, this route's destination is the centre of São Vicente, so walk further down the narrow village road (street sign for 'Grutas').

Somewhat further down, the Caminho do Laranjal branches off from the Casa do Piedade. You could also take this old pilgrim's path to the Fátima chapel.

However, if you follow the street further downhill, you soon come to the car park **12** for the **São Vicente cave**. An underpass leads below the express road to the caves' entrance area, which has a café and souvenir shop.

Walking further towards São Vicente, the street passes the fire brigade building (Bombeiros), which walkers only tend to notice when they've almost passed it. Keep left at the junction **13**. The church tower of São Vicente helps show the way: walk directly towards it. Bear slightly to the left at the following roundabout – heading directly towards the church tower.

Walk over a road bridge across the Ribeira de São Vicente. Beyond this is a car park for the centre of the village; walk diagonally across it. On the other side, it meets the old regional road **14** to the Encumeada pass.

A few metres further on, there is a bus stop on the left – though the buses here don't run via the Encumeada pass. If you're travelling back to the starting point, bear right after the car park; there is another bus stop just a few steps further on. From here, bus line 6 departs at about 15.30 and travels back to Funchal via the Encumeada pass and Ribeira Brava.

Walk past the bus stop; the street also passes the town hall square (Largo de Municipio). Continue ahead with the square to your left and then turn left into the next street to reach the central taxi rank. A few metres further on is the main entrance to the church **15**. You could also stop for a bite to eat at Bar/Café Estoril. ◾

Nature route

Up to waypoint 7, the route leads through **natural laurel forest**. The man-made path aside, this area has barely been touched by humans. Further below, almost at the end of the route, you pass the **São Vicente caves** 13, the only volcanic caves open to visitors on Madeira. Guided visits only, daily 10am–6pm except 25 Dec. Entry €8.

*** Through the enchanted forest by Fanal

This path leads through a unique, primeval landscape on the north-east slope of the Ribeira da Janela – the longest river on Madeira. The walk features sweeping views of dark-green slopes covered in dense, natural vegetation. Magnificent ancient laurel trees stand at the start of the path.

▶▶ The access road to the country lodge ends at a chain that blocks off the road. You can park here **1**. A first impressive specimen of a Madeira stinkwood laurel tree stands tall just beside the parking area. Walk past the **country lodge** keeping it to your right. Dirt steps rein-

An early earthy section

forced with wooden beams come into view up ahead. At the foot of the steps, a sign points to the footpath ('Paúl da Serra, 8 km'). Your climb starts here.

At the top of the steps, keep right and walk further to the east along a meadow path. Follow it along a slope that falls away to the north. In foggy conditions – which are common here – it's easy to lose the path, so a GPS device is certainly useful. However, the route soon comes to a clear beaten path. After a good 10 minutes, the path bends slightly to the left and you walk along past tall heather bushes. A little later, the path descends into an **enchanted laurel forest**. The knotted old trees are covered in lichens, mosses and ferns. It's quite easy to lose your way as you admire and photograph the captivating surroundings and forget the walk. The wooden beams supporting the path show that you're on the right track. Heather bushes soon join the laurel trees, ▶

Length/walking time: approx. 13.4 km, 4:05 hrs (7.9 km, 2:35 hrs without walking back).

Terrain: carefully constructed path through the humid laurel forest. Some dirt and rock steps must be crossed. Surefootedness required in wet conditions. The walk back to the start follows a quiet, rarely used road on the edge of the plateau 12.

Marking: red-yellow markings and signs. The footpath is officially called PR 13 'Vereda do Fanal'. Red and white signs mark the hunting ground border – don't mistake them for route markings!

Equipment: rain and wind protection should always be in your backpack. Some statistics show that the Paúl da Serra plateau sees About 300 days of fog per year. A **GPS receiver** is therefore a good idea.

Supplies: take everything, nowhere to buy food or drink for miles around.

Getting there: only possible by car, no public transport connections. The starting point is by the country lodge Posto Florestal Fanal on the ER 209 Ribeira da Janela – Paúl da Serra. If you approach from the south, 'Fanal' is signposted on the plateau. Driving from the north, you firstly pass the 'Fanal' picnic area (large sign). The next turnoff then leads to the country lodge.

Walk 37

▶ and the path comes to a wide forest track that was created to help fight forest fires.

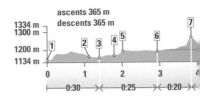

The track soon becomes a meadow path once again. A corrugated iron hut **2** appears on the left after a short descent. The path veers right at this point, and a sign points the way. At a subsequent fork where the now wide meadow path bends to the right, keep left and continue along a narrow beaten path. Use a weathered cairn to find your way.

The path snakes through heather bushes two to four metres high. A little later, it comes to another track **3** on which you bear right ('Paúl da Serra, 6.7 km'). Even if you missed the fork by the weathered cairn, you'll still reach the same track.

Then continue walking south-west, though you soon leave the track to the left (signposted) **4**. A narrow path rises gently at first, but soon becomes steeper with steps in places.

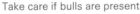

Take care if bulls are present

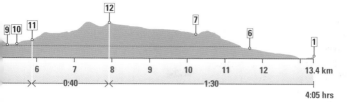

After a brief climb, you come across a forest path **5** crossing yours. Follow it further up to the left ('Paúl da Serra, 6.1 km'). After a few minutes, pass a lovely **viewpoint** to the left with a view of the wild, dark-green vegetation of the north coast

Shortly after the viewpoint, you come to a fork in the path; keep left and follow the main track. Keep left again at a subsequent fork where another track leads down to the right. A right-hand bend then follows and leads to regional road ER 209 **6**. If you've had enough, you can stop here as the little-used road soon returns to the starting point.

The path only touches the road, and does not cross it at this point. An idyllic section follows through tall tree heath and heather woodland, with unobstructed views of the north coast's dark green slopes every now and then. ▶

Walking through the enchanted forest

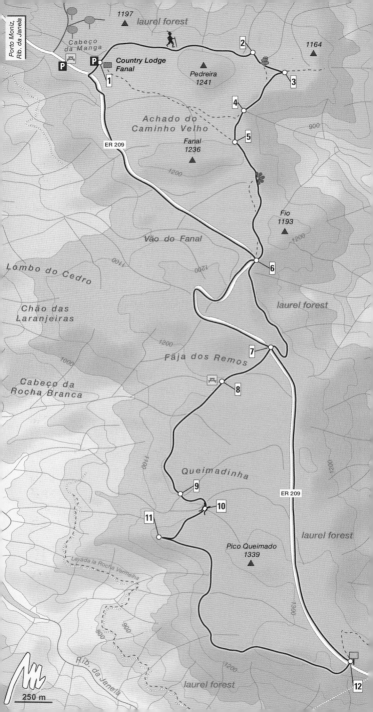

▶ After the heather bushes, you walk through mystical laurel forest once again. Some 15 minutes after the road, your route bends up to the right. (Footprints leading straight on here might confuse you.)

A steep climb ends at the ER 209 **7** once again. This point offers another opportunity to shorten the route and return along the road back to the start.

On the other side of the road, continue into the forest ('Paúl da Serra 4.1 km'). Steps supported with wooden beams head down into the laurel forest and lead walkers to a small, secluded picnic area **8** with a table and benches – a good spot for a break.

After this, the path rises gently once again. The onward path undulates somewhat through tree heath, heather and broom bushes. Soon after, a view of the slopes of the Ribeira da Janela river opens up to the right. The river's mouth is on the north coast at a location that shares the same name, in the vicinity of Porto Moniz.

The path crosses a photogenic tributary **9** and then runs along the slope down to the Ribeira da Janela river. A wooden bridge spans another small side valley **10** before a short, sharp climb.

> ### Route composition
>
> The official PR 13 footpath is a one-way route and is logistically difficult for individual walkers. The route described here limits itself to the most enjoyable parts of the route. The return journey back to the start is along the road. However, the road sees very little traffic and offers a variety of views and scenery. There are opportunities along the route to shorten the walk at **6** (total walking time 1:20 hr) and **7** (total walking time 2:15 hrs).

At the top, you have the option of a short detour to a viewpoint **11** to the right (sign at the fork: 'Miraduro').

The main path then continues to the south. Paths leading to the ER 209 regularly branch off and down to the left.

Just before the end of the route described here, there is one final, fairly tough climb to do, though it doesn't take long and then a few stepped sections lead downhill. There are frequent scenic views stretching to the source region of the Ribeira da Janela river and Rabaçal to the right.

After a left-hand bend, the path reaches the ER 209 **12**. This route ends here. The path does continue on the other side of the road; however, you've already seen the most interesting sections. The route back to the start follows the ER 209 road, which is rarely used in the afternoon. Perhaps you'll be lucky and find a day-tripper happy to take one more in the car.

If not, the walk along the road back to the start is a good 5 km. It leads gently downhill the whole way, so you'll return to Fanal in just under 1:30 hr. ■

Descent from Eagle Rock

Index

Map legend

Symbols

🔋 Tower

🕯 Lighthouse

📡 Radio mast

△ Campsite

🏖 Bathing beach

🏠◾ Building (serviced/general)

🏚 Mountain shelter

🏚 House ruins

🚩 Signpost

▲ Mountain summit

✝ Summit cross

🌿 Viewpoint

◠ Cave

🪨 Cliff

🌳🌿 Tree of significance

🖼 Rest area

☆ Natural attraction

🪨 Cairn

◌ Water basin

◍ Waterfall

◒ Spring

▢ Water basin

⊞ Gate

▦ Wall

Route guidance

🚶 Walking direction

⌀5 Waypoint with number

── Route

── Route

----- Variant/tunnel

i Tourist information

⛪ Monastery/convent

✝ Church

🏰 Castle

🏰 Castle ruins

▼ General attraction

★ Special attraction

∴ Archaeological site

🏛 Museum

⊹ Cemetery

⊕ Stadium

⊕ Harbour

✈ Airport

B Bus stop

T Taxi rank

P Car park

▬ Rail station

)(Bridge

( ) Tunnel

⊖ blocked

Water

▢ Water area

── River/riverbed

⋯⋯ Levada

Contour levels

▢ 0 to 200m

▢ 200 to 400m

▢ 400 to 600m

▢ 600 to 800m

▢ 800 to 1000m

▢ 1000 to 1200m

▢ 1200 to 1400m

▢ 1400 to 1600m

▢ above 1600m

100 / 001 Contour*

• Spot elevation

Streets and paths

▬▬ Motorway

▬▬ Trunk road

══ Main road

── Side road

── Track

= = = Tunnel

⊶⊶ Railway

■─■ Cable car

- - - Footpath

Locations

▢ Built-up area

● Settlement

All maps in this book are oriented to the north.
In 1:25,000 scale, 1cm on the map corresponds to 250m in reality;
in 1:50,000 scale, 1cm on the map represents 500m in reality.
*The contour line labels face upwards, i.e. out of the valley.